Praise for Mark Greenside's books

"An intimate portrait of an American expat who grapples with his mortality in a country that measures time by centuries, not minutes. Living in Brittany for 30 years—even if it's only part time—has fundamentally changed Greenside, just as it's done for all of us who are fortunate to call France home. After reading *I'm Finally,* Finally *French*, you may find yourself tempted to make an offer on the home that's up for sale next door to Greenside's cozy abode."
—Craig Carlson, author of *Pancakes in Paris* and *Let them Eat Pancakes*

"A bicontinental life with more pratfalls than a Jerry Lewis movie."
—Christine Muhlke, *The New York Times*

"Failure to speak French has never been so funny! Greenside may never master the gender of French nouns, but he sees straight through the French. A smart, delicious memoir of life off the beaten track in France."
—Julie Barlow, author of *The Bonjour Effect*

"Learning how to shop, drive, and eat in France have their own sets of rules, and *(not quite) Mastering the Art of French Living* tackles them with a soupçon of humor. From buying a lamp to mastering mollusks (oysters), and learning the right—and wrong ways—things are done in France, Mark Greenside perseveres . . . and succeeds."
—David Lebovitz, author of *My Paris Kitchen*

"Mark Greenside recounts hilarious experiences only a foreigner can have in France, for they're the ordinary things of French life that go unnoticed by the locals yet the funniest of things for someone from the 'outside'!"
—Susan Herrmann Loomis, author of *On Rue Tatin*

"Mark Greenside does an exceptional job of describing the many fish-out-of-water moments of life abroad. He also writes movingly about how his experiences in a new land have changed him. This is a book not to be missed!"
—myfrenchlife.org

"Surely the funniest American to land in France since Jerry Lewis, Greenside 'masters' the baffling rules of French life in principle, while mangling them—to hilarious effect—in practice. A delightful pas de deux of humor and wisdom."
—William Alexander, author of *Flirting with French*

"You cannot read this book without thinking about spending a delicious slice of life in France."
—Aileen Bordman, author of *Monet's Palate Cookbook*

"Hilarious . . . Reminds me of Stephen Clarke's books with its astute observations, wit, and affection for France."
—Ann Mah, author of *Mastering the Art of French Eating* and *The Lost Vintage*

"A hilarious look at trying to navigate life in France, literally and figuratively."
—Michelle Richmond, author of *The Year of Fog*, *The Marriage Pact*, and *Golden State*

"Thoughtful, heartfelt, and really, really funny."
—Keith Van Sickle, author of *One Sip at a Time: Learning to Live in Provence*

"One of the nicest of the trillions of books about France."
—Diane Johnson, author of *L'Affaire*, *Le Mariage*, and *Le Divorce*

"This tale of how one man accidentally becomes a thoroughly integrated member of a French village is funny, insightful, and winningly self-deprecatory. (My favorite character may be the nervous insurance agent.) And Mark Greenside's version of rudimentary spoken French is actually a good demonstration of how to communicate in a language you don't know!"
—Lydia Davis, author of *Varieties of Disturbance: Stories* and translator of *In Search of Lost Time* by Marcel Proust

"A light, lighthearted, occasionally very funny romp through a region of France not well represented in the travel literature. With his fresh eye and self-deprecating wit, Greenside sketches a wry, cautionary tale for all those of us who are tempted by adventures in foreign real estate."
—Michael Sanders, author of *From Here, You Can't See Paris: Seasons of a French Village and Its Restaurant*

"Mark Greenside has written a sweet, evocative book about the pleasures and perplexities of buying and owning a house in a small town in France. It's a funny, enlightening journey. Sit back, relax, and enjoy the trip."
—Richard Goodman, author of *French Dirt: The Story of a Garden in the South of France*

I AM FINALLY, *FINALLY* FRENCH

I AM FINALLY, *FINALLY FRENCH*

My Accidental Life in Brittany

Mark Greenside

Skyhorse Publishing

Skyhorse Publishing books may be purchased in bulk at special discounts for sales promotion, corporate gifts, fund-raising, or educational purposes. Special editions can also be created to specifications. For details, contact the Special Sales Department, Skyhorse Publishing, 307 West 36th Street, 11th Floor, New York, NY 10018 or info@skyhorsepublishing.com.

Skyhorse® and Skyhorse Publishing® are registered trademarks of Skyhorse Publishing, Inc.®, a Delaware corporation.

Visit our website at www.skyhorsepublishing.com.

Please follow our publisher Tony Lyons on Instagram @tonylyonsisuncertain.

10 9 8 7 6 5 4 3 2 1

Library of Congress Cataloging-in-Publication Data is available on file.

Cover design by David Ter-Avanesyan

Print ISBN: 978-1-5107-8397-3
Ebook ISBN: 978-1-5107-8400-0

Printed in the United States of America

To

Dorothy and Ernie Greenside, my parents, and
Esther, Joe, Rose, and Sandor, their parents, and
Donna Umeki, the love of my life, and
the residents and friends in Plobien, Brittany, and France.

Words are not enough.

Note to the Reader

Plobien and Loscoat, the names of the villages, and some of the people's names are fictionalized. Everything else in this story is true.

Contents

Foreword

I first came to Brittany thirty years ago with a girlfriend, but after a few weeks together she and I fell out of love with each other, and I fell in love with the place: its heathered hills, North Sea light, gargantuan tides, white sandy beaches, planetarium night skies, and kind, curious, *thankfully* welcoming people. Then, because love makes you crazy and do crazy things, I did one of the most scary and improbable things in my life. I, who don't speak French, don't like to fly, had no money, who owned only an eighteen-year-old Volvo and the clothes in my closet, borrowed money from my mom, and without a single inspection, on the word of the owners, bought a 120-year-old used-to-be farmhouse in Plobien, the village where my girlfriend and I rented a house. I thought it was the most daunting and terrifying thing I'd ever done. It wasn't.

The most daunting thing was "Now that I'm here, what do I do?" How do I learn the ropes and untie the knots of day-to-day life, which works well for most French people, but not so well for me, such as: what do I do when I have a car accident and it *is* my fault; how do I get my money out of *my* bank;

what do (and don't) I feed a French person I've invited to dinner; and most importantly, in which stores and from what vendors can I and can't I touch the tomatoes?

It turns out that was NOT the most daunting part of my life. It's now, when, for the first time in my life, I have a sense of an ending. . . .

I was forty-seven when I borrowed money from my mom and bought the house in Plobien. I had lots of expectations and fears at the time: replacing the roof, septic tank, and furnace; never learning French; having to fly ten hours to get to Paris; not enough money, not enough friends, knowing nothing about maintaining a house, yard, trees, and garden. I imagined grand parties and fêtes, living here thirty, forty, or fifty years, but I never worried, thought about, or expected to be thirty years older. *That* was beyond my imagination—and so was finally becoming French.

I'm the same person I was when I bought the house, only older, grayer, balder, thinner, and quieter. I'm healthy, active, and very regular, with less physical wear and tear than most people. (Mental wear and tear is something else.) I'm old enough now to know life is a crap (and for too many people a crappy) shoot, and that I've drawn the luck of the draw—so far. I don't know how long that luck will last, but if it's true, as experts say, that facing new challenges (and not being killed by them) enhances the brain and prolongs living, I'm going to be the smartest old guy in France, or the oldest smart guy: the French Methuselah. Time will tell—and so will I.

I

Brittany is pretty and it's not far from France.
—Coluche

Déjà Vu and Déjà New

I arrive at the house, as always, expecting everything to be as it was when Donna and I left (déjà vu), knowing we've been away nine months and everything changes (déjà new). You'd think by now I'd know better, but I don't. Even changes I initiate myself surprise me.

For years, the shutters on my house were white. They were white when I bought the house, and they were white after each of the three times I repainted. For all I know, they have only and always been white—150 years of whiteness—as most of the houses in Plobien and Brittany. So last year, when Rick, my friend, contractor, and all-material fixer-upper, said, "It's time to repaint," I didn't think twice. I like the clean, pure, satin whiteness of the wood against the craggy blacks, browns, blues, and grays of the granite and slate walls—and I like that white is vintage, even old, and resists the invasion of the new Provençal colors of sand, egg, apricot, and peach. So when Rick said, "It's time to repaint," I said, "Keep everything as it is," consciously upholding the tradition of white, albeit an English

white, because Rick and before him Martin, both British arti-
sans, told me French paint is crap.

And that's what would have happened if not for Donna.
For her, painting means new and different; it means color; it
means change, things I resist to the bone. How my politics
can be change-the-world left-liberal radical when everything
about me is leave-me-alone conservative is one of the mysteries
of my life, and probably why I long ago abandoned Sartre and
Mao and embraced Camus, and why I want to keep my shutters white.

I know Donna would relent and accept white if I pushed
it. *That's* not the problem. The problem is she's usually right.
When we were painting the California house—*her* house, the
house she bought years before we were married—I was ada-
mant about white walls. The house is a pre-1906 earthquake
modified Queen Anne with lots of windows and eleven-foot
ceilings. I wanted white walls to maximize the light: white
walls, white ceiling, white moldings, white doors. As in most
things like this, she ignored me. She wanted color, change, déjà
new. You'd think since it's her house, *I'd* relent, but I didn't.

"You can't go wrong with white," I said, "can't go wrong"
apparently becoming the chief motivator and lowest common
denominator in my life.

"Let's get it right," Donna responded—and right there,
once again, is the difference between us: half-empty and half-
full, Jewish and Buddhist. *That* story.

A few days later, on the day before I was leaving for Plobien
for our mutually agreed upon best-for-each-other alone time, I
walked into the living room and saw swatches of paint on the
walls—not one of them white, and not one I liked. There was a
sickly green, like mucus; a yellow-orange, like tobacco-stained

teeth; beige-ish-brown, like hospital walls; dark brown, like dookey. The only color I liked was a cream or sand or ecru or eggshell that was close to white, but wasn't. I expressed my preference and left for Plobien, where shortly after I arrived Donna sent me photos of the house. The walls were celadon, wheat, corn, and gorgeous. . . . They gave me pause. They still do. So when she arrived a month later and said, "I think you should paint the shutters green," after I told Rick to paint them white, I listened.

I also asked my friend Sharon, who is a painter, and she said, "Why not?" I asked her husband, Jean, a writer and filmmaker who has an opinion about everything, and he didn't disagree, which is as positive as he gets. I asked Rick and his wife, Ella, and everyone else I know, and they all said green was okay—but which green? There are dozens of shades on the internet and a chartreuse house on the quay. Clearly, if you can't go wrong with white, you can with green.

The rest of the summer Donna and I drove around observing the colors of shutters (mostly white) and taking photos of different greens—absinthe, artichoke, lime, leek, celery, moss, olive, Granny Smith, pistachio, mint—until finally, doubtfully, queasily, certain I was making a mistake and ruining the house, the village, and Breton tradition, I settled on forest green, because Donna said, "It works best. It complements the trees around and behind the house."

"There's been a change," I told Rick. "The shutters get painted forest green," and I showed him a photo of a house with forest green shutters and handed him a sample color swatch a few days before Donna and I left for California.

Over the next nine months, I sent him multiple emails—for birthdays, anniversaries, holiday greetings, thanks, get-wells, hellos, and how-are-you, and in each one mentioned the forest green shutters, concluding with, "I think they're going to look great. I can't wait to see them." And now, after twenty-three hours of travel, I'm sitting in my car, parked in the driveway, looking at the forest green shutters, and I'm shocked that they're not white.

They look good, and they do complement the trees around and behind the house, but they're new, and I'll have to get used to them—at least until the next time Rick paints and I go back to white . . .

I step out of the car, breathe deeply, and smell the grass. Monsieur Charles cut it for my arrival. I smell it before I see it. Two doves flap out of a tree, swoop up, land on the chimney, and start coo-cooing, either courting or warning the avian world, "He's here." I follow the slate path to the stone shed where Madame P's garden tools and my dying, Monsieur C life-supported furnace reside and continue walking the perimeter of the yard to see what else has changed: stone wall tumbling a little more; more dead branches in the apple tree; Madame P's garden smaller this year than the year before. On the other side of the house, the west side story, Rick has repainted the terrace white; Monsieur Charles buttressed the sagging wooden fence; the bay tree is pungent, ready for soups, and the quince is healthy and well on its way to becoming *confiture* . . .

At the front door, I jiggle the key into the lock and turn it carefully, easily . . . once. I turn it again, and it jams. I've been meaning to replace this lock for years. I don't because I also plan to replace the door, which is old and warped and out of alignment, and frequently gets stuck on the 130-year-old tile floor. I don't replace the door because I like the 1920s floral design grillwork that covers the two frosted glass windows that are supposed to open but don't, because long before me and Martin and Rick, someone painted the latches shut. To loosen them risks breaking the windows and damaging the grille. So the latches remain sealed, the windows shut, the door sometimes sticks—especially when it rains—and the lock is a continuing pain.

I pull the door toward me and turn the key. It unlocks, and I see Ella's been here: the tile floor in the hallway is gleaming, and the six-by-ten-foot red-and-black kilim that I carried to France in a suitcase back when baggage was unlimited and free has been vacuumed.

I take off my shoes and go into the kitchen. A vase of lilies and red roses sits on the Lemon Pledged—I smell it—oak parquet table the previous owners left for me. Surrounding the vase are Ella's folder of bills for the year, a bottle of Muscadet, and a welcome card—*Bienvenue Marc*—from Madame P. I open the kitchen window and shutters, and that shimmering midday North Sea light I fell in love with the first day I was in Brittany fills the room, though it's seven o'clock in the evening.

The stove gleams in the light. My new stove. That's how I think of it, even though it's more than ten years old. It replaced the stove Jean fixed with a slice of tin from a can of corn twenty years ago. The old stove scared me because every time I turned it on, I thought it would explode. The new stove scares me because it is computerized, and I'm afraid I, by mistake, or someone seeking a culinary adventure will turn the little knob on the central panel and change the preprogrammed setting, and I'll never be able to use the oven again. I once asked Sharon how to work it. She looked at it, read the instructions—which are in every European language except English—looked at it again, and said, "Leave it alone," which I have faithfully done.

I plug in the fridge. The new fridge, because the old fridge, the one that came with the house when I bought it, was stolen. Stolen! "Who in my village would do that?" I asked. "Roma," I was told. It's the all-purpose answer for anything that goes wrong. In the U.S., among my friends, the answer is Republicans. For others, it's liberals, immigrants, Democrats, Mexicans, Islamists, Muslims, Arabs, Jews, African Americans. *THEM.* Everyone has their short answer. Here, in Brittany, it's Roma.

In those days, Plobien had an annual fête on the third weekend in July—a Fête Nautique, a party on the river, with fireworks, rides, and a carnival. The people who ran the carnival were Roma. For two weeks every summer, they, with their Mercedes campers and cars, kids, dogs, and chickens, camped in the park across the street. They arrived a week before the fête began and stayed a week after it ended.

The campground is no longer there, and the fête is long gone, both the result of village cost cutting. The Romani are gone, too, but they were here a week before the refrigerator was stolen, so they were blamed.

I look around the kitchen, at the antique oak doors that cover the fireplace that once was for cooking, and now is a Martin-built cabinet to hide the dishwasher, microwave, and propane tank for the stove; the carved golden-oak antique breakfront I bought with my mom the first year I was here; the cabinets Rick built above the sink and the refrigerator; the faucet, replaced three times, first by Martin (with a French one), then Jean (a German one), and Rick (an Italian); the hand-painted HB-Henriot Quimper-ware ceramic clock Donna bought the first year she was here, the year of my fiftieth birthday party . . . .

I walk through the house, opening all the windows and shutters, letting that magical light pour in, looking at chairs, desks, lamps, beds, armoires, toilets, showers, the finished attic, sheets, towels, posters, floors, bookcases, books, remembering who, what, when, where, and why. . . . Everything has its story, and every story has its obstacles to overcome—*or not*—and a beginning, middle, and end . . .

"He's Here"

That's what I imagine François, my neighbor to the west, is thinking when he sees the shutters open on my house and my car—with its leased red, foreigner, license plates—in the driveway. He has lots of friends and family in the village and talks with everyone who passes by, except me. To him, my presence means another summer of not talking to his neighbor.

It's not that he actually wants to talk with me, it's that he thinks I'm rude because I don't talk to him. It's not that I don't want to talk with him, but he speaks so quickly, and makes no allowances for my idiocy—as everyone else does. To him, I've been here thirty summers, how could I not speak French? And then he speaks French to me, very fast, with a southern accent—because that's where he lived and worked before he retired and bought the house from his sister—and I feel even more idiotic. So we spend every summer with me avoiding him—just a wave and a "Bonjour" as I drive in and out of my driveway—and him thinking I'm rude.

Complicating things, I'm sure, are the many French people who regularly visit me and stay for hours, which, to him, must confirm my unneighborly rudeness. He must think, "He talks to them, why not me?"

I'd tell him why if I could: they don't care about, or no longer hear, or have completely given up on my lack of conjugation, terrible pronunciation, and misuse of gender. It's not that he's a grammarian, or that he cares, either, it's just that to his ears, I make no sense, which, of course, is the bottom-line truth. As my friend George once said to me, "You speak a French that no one else in the world would recognize as French." I do as well as I do—which isn't all *that* well—because most of the people I know make sense for me. My neighbor doesn't do that, or can't. The good news is I don't think he thinks I'm willful. The bad news is in twenty-plus years of living next to each other the only conversation we've had of any length or substance was the same conversation I had ten years earlier with his brother-in-law and niece about my cypress trees, only François demanded I cut them, and they let it go. But that was a long time ago, and we've long since worked it out (I cut a third of them, ten out of thirty). At this point, I think he would be happy to sit down over a Ricard—two geezers, he a retired cop, me a retired lefty professor—and chat about the old days, say May 1968. I would, too, but we both know it's hopeless. For me, it won't happen because I can't understand him. For him, because I'm rude.

"Il est là," I imagine he sighs to his dog. "He's here."

To Bruno and Françoise, my neighbors to the east, my arrival in Plobien means work. Actually, my *existence* in Plobien means work, as I'm only here two to three months a year, but they're working to help me year-round, as, for instance, in the spring when Françoise made multiple calls to get me the card I need to access the dump—*le déchèterie*—because I couldn't figure out how to do it.

For them, it's friendship, a neighborly duty, charity, international goodwill, and betting that good deeds in this life will make for a better afterlife, where hopefully their heavenly actions will no longer be needed.

For me, it's the passing of the torch to a new generation—from Madame P, who has been my primary caregiver for more than two decades, to Bruno and Françoise, who are fifteen to twenty years younger.

The good news is Bruno and Françoise *are* health providers. Bruno is a doctor, and Françoise is a nurse. Instinctively, they understand I need help, caring for, special treatment and assistance, reasonable accommodation to an unreasonable degree. Sometimes I feel I'm their private patient in my own personal ICU. If this is what's coming, it's not so bad.

When we travel together—as we often do—to Provence, Burgundy, Paris, the next village—they watch over me like parents with a two-year-old, as in, "What do you think he'll get into today, and how can we keep him from it?" To make sure I don't get lost, Françoise walks in front of me, Bruno behind. If they could put a name tag and leash on me, I'm pretty sure they would.

They have a son and a daughter and three young grandchildren, so they're well-versed and rehearsed in babysitting, intensive care, protective services, and initiating socialization skills, which in France includes toilet training (which thankfully I don't need—yet), table manners (which I do, such as when to eat with my hands and what to do with Bruno's perfectly grilled tripe sausage I won't touch), and language acquisition.

They even enlisted their four-year-old granddaughter, Naomi, to help me, probably thinking (1) our language skills are about equal (hers are better), and (2) she'd be more patient than they (though they are as patient as granite—and she's not). The first time I spoke French with her, she looked at me like, "Is this a joke?" Then at Bruno and Françoise like, "Is he from Belgium?" Then back at me like, "You're an old guy, how can you be so stupid?" It's a question I often ask myself.

Once, after a delicious meal that Bruno cooked, I said, "C'est délicieux," pronouncing it "delishoe."

Naomi corrected me, "delissue."

"Delishu," I repeated.

She repeated, "delissue."

"Delichew," I said.

She stared at me, trying to decide if I was being funny, teasing her, or I really was an idiot. Françoise pulled her away before she could decide. Though I think by now she has.

The good news is Erine, their other granddaughter, is learning English, and *she* thinks I'm a genius—though I don't think she's told Naomi. Victor, Erine's brother, just ignores me, which is probably the safest and smartest response.

For Bruno and Françoise, my presence means another summer of lesson plans—take him here, show him this, teach him something. What complicates things is my age. I'm older than they, and at some point they will have to determine if or when my cultural failures become biological, when one elides into the other, and what to do about it.

I call them a few days after I arrive, and they invite me to their house, where Bruno opens a bottle or two of wine. For years, I thought it was to celebrate our getting together again. Lately, though, I've been thinking it's also self-medication, to reduce their anxiety about me. When Donna's here, she speaks French, and is responsible. When she's not here, which is half the time, it's left to Madame P, Jean and Sharon, Gilles and

Tatjana, and Bruno and Françoise—and since they're closest—
right next door—and friends *and* health professionals, they
worry about their responsibility a lot.

Bruno puts three glasses on the table along with bowls
of chips, nuts, tiny cheese squares, olives, sliced chorizo, and
bottles of red, white, and whiskey, and calls, "Bonjour Mark,"
when a few days later I knock on their door.

For Madame P, my first friend and taliswoman—who I
now sometimes call Yvonne because a few years ago she insisted
I do even though she'll always be Madame P to me—my
arrival means camaraderie, as her garden and world have gotten smaller. She has good friends and neighbors, four grandchildren, four great-grandchildren, and Henri, her younger
son, but everyone works or goes to school and is in one way or
another productive, while I go to the beach and sit home not
doing much that anyone can see. Yes, I'm a writer, and writers are revered in France—thank God—but what's a book a
decade compared to Balzac, Zola, Proust, and Sartre?

From day one in Plobien, I've depended on her for help,
advice, direction, and assistance, and she's selflessly given
them. To thank her and return the favors, I call her whenever I
go shopping, and ask, "Je vais shopping. J'achète quelque chose
pour vous?" I go shopping. I buy something for you?

Mostly, she answers "Non merci" but sometimes—I think
to make me feel good and useful—she says "Oui." She always
keeps it simple and minimal—three slices of ham, bread, two
peaches—because more often than not I bring her not exactly
what she wants: the wrong ham, whole-grain bread instead of
white, white peaches instead of yellow.

Lately, she's been saying "Oui" more frequently, and sometimes she even calls me—to drive her to a doctor's appointment,

pick up medicine at the pharmacy, or take her to the weekly market in Loscoat. The things I do for her are simple, easy, mechanical. The things she does for me are knowledge-based, skilled, and inspired. Plus, there's the success factor: anything I do for her has more than a modicum of a chance of not being right—like getting the wrong peaches; anything she does for me works out fine, the way I'd hoped, and often better.

She speaks French. I speak English and a French only my friends and shopkeepers who want to make a sale would even try to understand. She is a good Catholic, I'm a not-so-good Jew. Her politics are to the right of mine—how far to the right, I don't want to know. She's lived all her life in Brittany, the last fifty years in Plobien, a village of five hundred people. I grew up in New York and live in the San Francisco Bay Area—and here we are, linked for thirty years and counting.

When I arrive at the house there's always a vase of lilies, hydrangeas, and/or roses on the kitchen table, and a note telling me all is okay, she is okay, welcoming me back. If it's June or later, there's also a bag of veggies—onions, potatoes, zucchini, radishes, carrots from her garden. Sometimes there's an additional gift: a bottle of Breton cider from a farmer she knows; a new pen; a coffee cup with a Celtic design on it; homemade crêpes or *confiture*, the *pompiers* calendar—as if what she has given me the last thirty years isn't enough.

To Yvonne, my arrival closes the circle and her family is complete. She is the last person Donna and I visit when we leave, and the first person I call when I arrive. "Bonjour, Yvonne, c'est moi."

For Sharon and Jean my arrival means English. They speak French all year, then, when I arrive, they change their thought processes and language, and speak English—even to their

boys, who are French. With all my other bilingual friends—
Gilles, Tatjana, Bruno, Henri, Gaël, Marie, Albine—I speak
Franglish. With Sharon and Jean, it's English all the way.
Partially, I think, it's because Sharon is Canadian and English
is her first language, and partially because Jean can't bear to
hear my French without wanting to correct me, even though by
now he knows not to bother.

They—Sharon and Jean—are my first line of language
defense, and I utilize them often in the hope of avoiding or
mitigating offense. When an official letter arrives, say from my
bank, or an item appears in the village newsletter that looks
important—something about new recycling rules—I take it to
them for translation, after which I feel relieved (if they toss the
papers in the fireplace) or terrified (if even they don't know
what it means, or what I should do).

They work as a team, sometimes arguing, often agreeing,
always helping, or at least resolving—as in the time I handed
them a letter from the water company telling me I needed to
purchase inside-the-house leak insurance. Jean, who can fix
anything, read the letter and said, "It's crap, junk, a rip-off,"
and tossed it away. Sharon picked it up, read it, and said nothing, which might mean she agreed with him, and might mean
she didn't. I didn't buy the insurance, but every winter when
the house is closed I worry about the pipes freezing and wish
I'd bought it, and every summer, when I return and the pipes
haven't burst, I'm happy I didn't.

Over the years, Sharon and Jean have developed a highly
refined, time-tested division of labor—which means, depending on the situation, they work separately. When *I'll Never
Be French (no matter what I do)* was published in French, the
Maison de la Presse in Loscoat threw me a *dédicace*—which

I thought was something you do for a dead person. I showed Sharon and Jean the poster with a big picture of me and the book, announcing the time and the date of the event, and Jean immediately said, "I'm coming with you," and he did. He translated *and* spoke for me, and probably also explained, protected, and defended himself, as he is prominent in the book, and doesn't want another person (one already has) calling and asking him to fix her stove.

Jean is great with people and paper, but not so great with officialdom and authority, both of which make him angry and anxious. So when I said, "I made an appointment for Donna and me to meet with the *Notaire* to discuss trusts and wills, property ownership and estate taxes," Sharon said, "I'll go with you." That's how I learned France doesn't have trusts or recognize them, and my mother has more rights to the house than Donna.

Every year, there's something new: making an appointment with the tax office, contesting a parking ticket, finding someone to remove a wasp nest from the attic—and every year Sharon and Jean learn more and more about their world. I like to think that's my gift and contribution to their lives, even though I know it's a gift and contribution they don't need or desire.

Sharon always waits a few days after I arrive to invite me to dinner. She knows by now that I'll arrive on American time, the time she said, "8:00," not French time, thirty to forty minutes late—and she's ready, but the first twenty to thirty times it was awkward.

I pull the bell—a real bell—unlock the door using the secret method only they, their family, and I know, and follow the smells up the stairs into the kitchen, where Sharon stands over the stove, holding a pot or pan or fork—some cooking implement—she puts down to give me a hug and a two-cheek kiss, which I double and return with enthusiasm. The table is set, and next to Jean's place, ready for action, is his old, illustrated, beaten-up, stained, and creased Larousse dictionary.

"Jean!" Sharon calls, telling him this year's adventure in English is about to begin. "Mark's here."

For Tatjana and Gilles my arrival means games. Gilles is an elite school—*école supérieure de commerce*—graduate and Tatjana is Serbian, which means both of them expect to win, though I think Gilles expects it more than she does.

Sometime after I arrive, Tatjana emails their English-speaking friends, who are many, and Matthieu, who understands English perfectly, but refuses to speak it. He speaks a French that's so fast it makes my New York English sound like an Alabama drawl. The good news is he speaks this way to everyone. The bad news is they understand him, and I don't. Worse, he talks to me a lot.

On the appointed day, but never the appointed hour, we arrive at different times, food and drink in hand, ready for a yummy, *Auberge Espanoley* international potluck dinner followed by an Olympic-scale competition of word games, mind games, movement games, and memory games; games that are timed; games with teams; games with different teams: French Trivial Pursuit, French charades, French *Jeopardy!*, French Monopoly, French (not so simple) Simon Says, everything but French *The Price is Right*, which I'd probably do okay with.

Except for Matthieu, the games are played in English, ostensibly so I'll have a chance to win, but after losing for so many years, I now think it's so they can practice and hone their already well-practiced and honed English skills. Several, like

Tatjana, are ringers: English teachers, who understand the parts of speech and structure of English better than I ever will.

Albine, Yvette, Anne, Marie, and their husbands or boyfriends or both—I can't tell—are poised, ready, experienced, and expectant. The only one who doesn't care about losing is Matthieu. To him, these are only games. To everyone else, it's the U.S. vs. France (and maybe Serbia, too).

Tatjana emails everyone the date and time of this year's Olympic gathering. Everyone (except Matthieu), I imagine, plans on victory, while I prepare for defeat. As at Arles and Nimes in Roman times, the already vanquished provide the entertainment by finding new, ingenious, extraordinarily stupendous ways to succumb. In this regard, I never disappoint.

School is over. Mark is here. "Let the games begin."

To Monsieur Charles, who's been mowing my lawn and taking care of the trees and bushes and everything outside for twenty-five years, my arrival means unlimited Heinekens and payment for the work he has done all year. I don't tell him what needs to be done, and he doesn't ask. He just does it: pruning, cutting, cleaning, planting, watering—and if he can't do it, he knows someone who can. When I wanted a new cast-iron fireplace set in one of the two large living room fireplaces, he called his friend Monsieur L. When the remaining twenty trees François wanted me to cut fell down in a storm and had to be removed, he called Monsieur A; a new TV, Monsieur U. He always knows the right person, who will charge the right price, and do excellent work—just like him.

A day or an hour before I arrive, he cuts the grass. A few days later, he knocks on the door and says, "Bonjour."

"Bonjour, bonjour," I say, shaking his hand and adding a French air kiss and a California hug. "Entrez, entrez." I don't know why I repeat myself, but I do. Maybe to be sure I'm understood. He sits at the table, always in the same chair, with a view of the yard—the yard he knows better than I do. I don't drink much beer, but I always have a twelve-pack of Heineken in the fridge for Monsieur Charles. It's one of the first things I buy every year, and about the only thing I never run out of.

"Voudrais vous un biére?" I ask.

"Oui," he says, as if it's a great idea, and the first time I ever asked. I set two glasses on the table, open a chilled bottle and pour slowly, as I know he wants me to do. I fill my glass with orange juice—and we sit there, chatting about the weather, the yard, Madame P's garden, his health, my health, the world's health, and his latest version of Whac-A-Mole—with fire, smoke, water, piercing mole-deafening sounds, chemicals, firecrackers, and once, a rifle. He's always kind and funny, amused by everything around him, except the moles. We've been doing this for so long now he's become accustomed to my bastard French and understands me, often better than I do. If other people are present, he'll translate me into French-French, so they too can understand what I mean, not what I say. I like to think he thinks of my French as "American" French, much the way French people think of Canadian French as "Québécois." For me, this arrangement works fine, but when Donna arrives and speaks to him in French-French, he looks at me for translation, and Donna, who has been studying and practicing French all year, looks at me, annoyed.

He never stays more than thirty minutes, and never has more than one beer. When he leaves, he shakes my hand, and says, "A bientôt," see you soon, and he means it. Often, it's the following day.

For Ella and Rick, who replaced Christine and Jon, who replaced Martin and Louise, my arrival means closing the books for one year and opening them for the next.

When I arrive, Ella's yearly file folder is waiting for me with a welcome note and a bottle of wine. Inside the file are my bills for the past nine months—things she had to buy for the house: mostly cleaning supplies, sometimes repair parts, like for the furnace—and an itemization of the hours she spent cleaning the house and checking on it when it's closed. Next to her file is a separate file and list of Rick's work: making new kitchen cabinets; tiling the bathroom floor; building a new shower; repairing cracked windows; replacing old sockets; rewiring. I file their files in my file, write a check, and give it to them the first week I'm here, happily knowing as I hand it to Ella that she's already begun a new file, and we're continuing for another year.

For Eric and Manu, my arrival means unbillable time. Every year, when I leave, I shut the computer down and put it away, which means every year when I return the software is at least a year's worth of Windows and Word updates behind. Mostly, they update themselves automatically when I boot up, but sometimes they don't, and sometimes one web browser— say, Mozilla, which has worked fine for years—no longer works with the newest upgrade and has to be switched to Chrome, a switch I have no idea how to do. There can also be modem problems, phone line problems, and problems with the plugs, each of which brings me to Eric and Manu. They could bill me for all of this work—they *should* bill me for all this work—but they rarely do. To thank them, I buy all of my computer supplies at their shop even though they probably wish I didn't, because (1) they usually don't have what I need (because it's out-of-date); (2) they have to order it (which takes time); and (3) we all know I could get it cheaper, faster (and easier for them) at the *supermarché*.

For Fred at the Maison de la Presse, my arrival means selling out of sunny picture postcards of Plobien and ordering the *International Herald Tribune*, which no one in the village reads, except me. I buy all of my pen and ink and paper supplies from him.

I buy all of my cakes and tarts from Dominique and Michelle, the fourth-generation baker and his English mate, at the same patisserie where the third generation—his dad—made my fiftieth birthday party cake.

The oil guy's son, Eric, still provides my fuel.

Claude and Annie are no longer surprised when I show up at their office unannounced and ask my latest insurance questions—about floods, fallen trees, potential broken pipes—or pay my bill a month early so it won't be late.

The *Notaire* acts as if it's normal for an illiterate foreigner to make yearly appointments to discuss how to avoid French laws about trees and inheritance taxes.

I buy my veggies from the same *légumerie*, my *poulet, porc*, and *boeuf* from the same *boucherie* (second owner), my raisin-nut bread (*noix de raisin*) from the same boulangerie (third owner).

The *Poste* lady in Loscoat still cringes when I open the door.

Once a year Donna and I eat dinner with Hugo and Martine, Jean-Pierre and Joëlle, Béatrice and Jean-Jacques, and Henri and René and their families, alternating from their houses to ours on about a 3:1 ratio, three at theirs, one at ours, as they are all better cooks than us.

A few years ago—for the first time in twenty-six years—I didn't go to France. Donna's work schedule was awful, making her sick, and she couldn't leave. I decided I probably shouldn't go, either, a sacrifice I didn't know I had the ability to make until I made it. I wrote to everyone—except my neighbor François, figuring he wouldn't care, and the *Poste* lady, who I didn't want to make happy—and said, "Don't worry, all is okay, just busy, nothing wrong, but can't come to Plobien this year." I returned the following year and ever since life has been normal—French normal—where inexplicably, despite my deficits, local people and the Force are with me.

I wish I could say the same about technology.

Agent Orange

My smartphone makes me feel dumb. . . . I remember, not that long ago, when I could work all of my appliances. I didn't understand *how* they worked, but I could make them work: TV, dishwasher, stove, washing machine, the control knobs on my old Volvo. Now, I'm a touch away from disaster. Push the wrong button, turn the wrong knob, touch the wrong icon, and it's worse than HAL in the movie *2001*. There, Dave knows what he's doing and outfoxes HAL, but me, I haven't a clue. The one thing I have learned, though, is after something goes wrong to not push, turn, or touch anything else, because as bad as things are, they will only get worse, and I'll get frustrated and further away from where I want to be: say, streaming, or using the eco-natural, energy-saving dry cycle on my dishwasher; doing a semidry/semi-load of laundry with a hot wash and cold rinse.

In my younger days, I thought nothing about my appliances. They were there and did their jobs until they broke. Then I called the Sears or Maytag or KitchenAid repairman—it was always a man—and he'd fix it, and after another five, ten, or twenty years, I'd replace it with the same machine.

Now, I live in fear of my appliances, knowing if anything goes wrong or the settings change or, God forbid, they break a week after the warranty runs out, I'm done for: first, because customer service has become a forty-plus-minute wait on the phone listening to a recorded voice telling me every ten seconds how important my call is to them; second, because whomever I speak to will (a) know nothing; or (b) not be able to do anything, as the company that made the product, and the company that sold the product, and the company that delivered the product, and the company that installed the product, no longer repairs the product, and no longer has a repair department; and/or (c) try to convince me the failure isn't with their product, but with another product that is necessary to run their product, as, for instance, when I call Xfinity because I want to stream a show and I can't, because the modem Xfinity gave me doesn't work.

I know it's the modem because the Xfinity repair guy who arrived three hours late to repair something else took pity on me and spent another forty-five minutes—going to his truck three times, and opening the modem and breaking the code— to connect me. It worked fine for a while, then it didn't.

I called Xfinity, and after a twenty-minute wait, said, "I can't stream. Your modem won't let me stream."

"Sir, I just did a check. Your modem is fine."

"I know it's not. The Xfinity guy who fixed it told me the new modems are terrible and cause all kinds of problems."

"I don't see a record of Xfinity repairing your modem."

"I know it's the modem."

"Sir, I just ran a test. It's your TV."

I call Samsung, wait thirty minutes, and say, "Xfinity said my TV is broken. It won't connect to my modem."

I wait another thirty minutes while they run a zillion more tests, knowing exactly what they're going to tell me: "It's not the TV, it's the modem."

So I sit here with a TV that's not as smart as it thinks it is and a modem that connects with the TV when it wants to. I live with it because it's a TV, an ancillary instrument in my life. When it's my computer, it's a problem of a different magnitude. When it's my computer, I'd be lost without my friend and techie guru, Bob, a self-taught computer magician who so far has been able to fix anything that needs fixing. That's in the U.S. In France, it's Eric and Manu, two guys I only recently met.

In the U.S, my writing office—the office I rent—is a three-room suite on the second floor of a locked building where I have no telephone or internet access, because I do not wish to be connected, reached, or in any way disturbed by the outside world. There's plenty of time for that in the rest of my life. I feel that even more strongly about my time in France: why come to France to live like I do in the U.S.?

For the first dozen and a half years, I resisted. Then one day out of the blue—out of *my* blue—Donna says, "I can't stay in Plobien for six to eight weeks without being connected."

Merde. I know what this means: compulsively reading Giants scores, baseball stats, and the news; hearing from and obsessively responding to people I don't want to hear from or respond to; watching YouTube; googling, Yahooing, Amazoning, and eBaying; living my American life in France. I also know what will happen if I don't . . . .

Amazingly, a computer store recently opened in Loscoat. When I first saw it, I was disappointed, seeing it as another invasion of the new into the perfectly fine old. Now, it seems to be a sign from the gods. If Loscoat is ready for this, then I am, I think, conveniently forgetting that French people love novelty and technology, and I don't. So after I unpack, shop for food, check my bank account, and settle in, I take my laptop to the new computer shop in town and say, "Bonjour."

A tall, thin, wiry guy with dark curly hair and a twinkle in his eyes—which could be friendly amusement, menacing anger, or turn either way in an instant—greets me with a smile and a frown. I haven't spoken yet so I can't figure out why the frown. The store is new and no one else is there, you'd think he'd want the business. I start to explain that I need a modem for the internet.

"Monsieur, avez-vous le modem pour le internet?"

He looks around the shop. There are piles of modems everywhere.

"Oui."

"Bon," I say, and hand him my computer. He looks at me as if a Cro-Magnon man entered his shop and started speaking.

"This is old," he says.

"You speak English?"

He says, "Yes, of course." Like, didn't you just hear me?

I tell him that I live in Plobien and have been coming here every summer for twenty years (so he knows I'm a regular and a neighbor and he'll see me again); that I'm a writer, because I know it's a good thing to be in France (but I don't tell him about *I'll Never Be French*, because I don't want him to worry or even think about what I might write about him, because I haven't yet learned *to* tell him so he *will* worry and think about what I'll write about him); that I never wanted to be online because it's distracting—no need to tell him I have no willpower or self-control—but, "My wife insists, *insistes!* [I emphasize in

French] that I connect this year *before* she arrives." I can see he's sorry he spoke to me in English.

He puts the computer on the worktable.

I say "Ici," and hand him the charger and power cords. Here.

He takes them and his frown deepens. He holds the cord in his hand and looks at me in disbelief. Shit. I left the adapter plug at the house, the plug that allows the three flat-pronged American plug to fit into the two round-hole French socket. I look around. This is a computer store, there must be an adapter plug somewhere. I don't see it, but I didn't see the modems, either, and they're everywhere. "Avez-vous le plug adaptor pour les États Unis?"

He closes his eyes and shakes his head, no.

I drive back to the house—fifteen minutes each way—get my adapter plug, and drive back. Luckily, the store is new, business is slow, and this guy—Eric—has less to do than I do, though hopefully he knows more than I do.

He takes the adapter, attaches it to the power cord, plugs it in, then plugs the other end into the computer and turns it on. He's staring at the computer, trying hard not to look at me or elicit anymore conversation while the machine takes forever to boot up.

"C'est lentement," I say. It's slowly.

"Ouiiiiiiiiiiiii . . ."

"C'est ancient." It's old.

He looks at me like, (1) I already know that, (2) you already said that, and (3) why are you talking to me in French?

Finally, it boots. I give him my password—*le passemot*—and he types it in and sees it's worse than he expected. The laptop is Donna's old one, at least six years old. I brought it to

France three years ago, meaning nothing has been updated for the past three years. He looks at me, lowering my Cro-Magnon status to Neanderthal.

"C'est bon pour internet, j'espère?" It's good for the internet, I hope.

"We'll see. Come back later today."

It's ten o'clock in the morning. I buy bread, eat lunch, and drive to Pentrez, my favorite pristine, white sand, mile-long beach and walk along the shore, letting the warm Gulf Stream waves lap at my feet—something I would never do in the northern California freezing Pacific. At four o'clock, I return to the shop. It's still customerless, and someone else is sitting at the front desk, a happy, friendly, content fellow with a man-in-the-moon Buddha-like face.

"Bonjour," I say. He responds so softly, I can hardly hear him, not that it matters, because it's French. "Je suis Monsieur Greenside."

"Eric," he calls. That's how I know the other guy's name is Eric.

Eric comes out of the back room, sees it's me, goes back to the back room, yells something to the person he'd rather be talking with, and comes out carrying my computer.

"C'est bon?" I ask.

He shrugs and explains that he updated all my files— Windows, Adobe Acrobat, Internet Explorer, who knows what else, maybe my writing as well; he cleaned out lots of junk files— hopefully not my writing—and added antivirus protection. He's done everything this old computer would allow. Now, it's ready for the internet. He's given me no indication of how long this took—five minutes or five hours—or how much it will cost. In the U.S., Bob does everything. Something fails (often it's me), I call him, he fixes it (unless it's me), I take him to dinner, then we go shopping and I buy him a digital toy, and that's that.

"You need a modem," Eric says, which is where I began. "You can buy," he points to the ones in the shop, "or rent," he lifts a box, "from Orange," the phone company. In the U.S., I own, which is what I'm about to do here, when Eric adds, "Orange has a special three-month sale."

Three months! Just the time I need it to keep Donna here and happy. "Bon," I say, "I'll rent."

The modem, called a Livebox, comes in a box. Inside the box are directions for setting it up and activating it, none of which I'd understand in English, but Eric, bless him, already knows this. He opens the box, asks for my phone number, makes a phone call, and we wait . . . and wait . . . and wait . . . fifteen minutes until someone finally answers. They talk for a few minutes, then Eric goes online—on *his* computer—and prints out my new Livebox contract with my name and password. All that remains is the installation, which unfortunately happens at the house, and is up to me.

Eric tells me where to plug the phone line, modem line, and power line into the Livebox. He tells me, shows me, and draws me a diagram. "In three or four days, you'll be activated. When you're finished, you return the Livebox to the Orange store in Quimper."

I pay him—less than thirty dollars for everything—and go home and follow everything Eric said and drew, and I wait. After five days, I'm still not connected.

I return to the shop, which is still customerless, and shout, "Bonjour!"

Eric comes out of the back room, sees it's me, and says, "Hello."

"Tout est bien, mais je n'aie pas la connexion." All's good, but I don't have the connection."

He goes online, taps in my phone number, and says, "This afternoon."

Two days later, I'm still not connected.

I go back to the store. This time Eric is talking with a customer. Ordinarily, I'd be upset that I have to wait, but I'm so happy he has another customer, I don't mind.

When the customer leaves, I tell Eric, "I'm still not online."

He repeats everything he's done before, and says, "Today."

I'm dubious, but I figure if Eric can't make this system work, neither Bob nor I would have a chance. I go to Leclerc to buy him a gift, then go home, and—voilà!—it works. I go back to the store to thank Eric *and* give him some good news for a change. As soon as he sees me, his face falls. He immediately starts typing on his keyboard. I feel bad. No one else gets this service, because no one else needs it, and I can see he's sorry he ever got into this.

"C'est marche," I say. "Tout est bien. Très bien. Merci, merci beaucoup," and I hand him a bottle of twelve-year-old Wild Turkey.

He's beaming. He's got the bourbon—*and* he's done with me.

I'm beaming. I have Wi-Fi! Soon Donna will be beaming. All is good in the world.

All summer the Wi-Fi works fine. The connection is terrific. Plobien, a village of five hundred people in rural France—as most of France—is well connected, and has been for years.

At the end of the summer, two days before we leave, I disconnect the Livebox and rebox everything—exactly as Eric told me—and drive to Quimper to return it to the Orange store, exactly as Eric told me, and to buy a new phone for Madame P, which she asked me to do.

After waiting in line for over an hour, a salesperson finally agrees to see me. He takes the box, checks that everything is inside, and signs, initials, and stamps all of the papers that verify: Livebox returned and all is okay. I buy Madame a new phone—one with large numbers, as she requested. I'm overjoyed. I'm already looking forward to next year. So is Donna. I can't say the same for Eric.

Two months later, back in California, I get a bill from Orange charging me the non-sale price for the Livebox I returned two months earlier. I call Sharon, who after two more months of being billed for a Livebox I no longer have, stops the billing. Eight months later I'm back in Plobien and planning to drive to Quimper and Orange to get my refund.

I'm trying to guess the best time to go and avoid the wait, which is like trying to figure out the fastest line in the supermarket or the quickest lane of traffic. It's hit and miss, and for me, in France, as elsewhere, it's mostly miss. Still, I have a plan.

Over the years, I've learned French people shop most often before lunch, from ten to twelve, after school and work, between five and seven, and on Saturdays, with the heaviest traffic occurring one hour before lunch and one hour after, and the lightest during lunch, between twelve and two, when most people in France stop whatever they're doing—except maybe surgery—to eat.

Factoring all of this in—and remembering when I'm on my way home from the beach at three or four o'clock, French people are arriving in squads—I decide to drive to Quimper at nine o'clock on a Wednesday morning, figuring the store opens at nine-thirty like most stores, and that no one is early for any-thing in France, except maybe death.

I drive to my latest secret parking place, which apparently is not secret anymore. I park next to the river, near the thir-teenth-century double-spired Gothic cathedral, where the Orange store is. This, I think, is a good omen. More and more, as I get older, I seek and find omens everywhere: first pitch a strike, the Giants will win; blood, sugar, cholesterol numbers okay, I'm good for another century.

I put three euros in the meter for two hours' parking, think-ing worst-case scenario, just in case. . . . I jaunt around the cor-ner and see a wedge of four people standing in front of the store. Pretty good, I think, proud of myself for getting it right. More and more, my French thinking is getting better and bet-ter. I get closer to the wedge of four and see another wedge of six people inside, also waiting, as this store apparently opens at nine o'clock, and at nine-o-five, which it is now, it's busy.

Five people are working in the store, but thanks to strict French division-of-labor rules, only two are actually talking to customers. The others are probably planning lunch or are on synchronized breaks or maybe are high school or college stu-dent summer interns. France is very good at providing part-time, seasonal jobs, which by the math alone should translate into better, quicker service, but doesn't.

I join the outside wedge of four, armed with my papers, the one thing I am never short of. My dad was a lawyer. I keep everything: tax records and receipts going back twenty years; contracts, policies, and warranties that expired decades ago; every paper I ever signed from my first day of employment to my last. And that's in the U.S. In France, I also keep letters, notes, advertisements—anything to prove this is what I did, or thought I did, or wanted to do, or intended—in case I agree to something I didn't intend. Not, I suppose, that it would matter. But this! This is clear. I have the signed, initialed, and stamped officiated and official Orange letter of receipt verifying that, yes, indeedy, I returned the Livebox last August and ended the three-month trial sale and canceled my service. I also have my bill from Orange and my bank statement showing they continued to bill me for another four months at the non-sale price. Voilà!

Meanwhile, the line hasn't moved. Everything takes forever. People in the wedge could speed things up if they went into the store and browsed and knew what they wanted when it was their turn, but if they did, they'd lose their place in the wedge. So they don't, meaning when it is their turn, they don't know what they want—or worse, they do know what they want, but the store doesn't have it, and worst, never will. The result is people do not begin to browse until it's their turn to be served by a salesperson—and while they are browsing, the salesperson, who could be working with someone else—me, for example!—is working with the browser while s/he figures out what s/he wants, changes his/her mind, or just plain loses it. Then, once a decision has been made, the same salesperson writes up the sale and passes the customer on to the next salesperson, who writes the sale up again, while another person goes off in search of the product, which sometimes they actually have.

One guy, I notice, is on his cell phone, standing next to a customer, saying nothing to the customer or the phone. He's been doing this for twenty minutes, so now there's only one salesperson working the wedge. There are no chairs, stools, or benches—old people, disabled, insane, and those going insane all have to stand and wait in the wedge.

One hour later, I'm still in the wedge, clutching my papers like a prescription for Vicodin, two people away from seeing a salesperson—unless they all suddenly go on a synchronized break. The woman with a cane, behind me, is faltering. In the U.S., I'd give her my spot, but here, in France, God knows what she wants—to rewire a twenty-five-room château—and I'll be here until Thursday. As usual, none of this seems to bother anyone, except me.

I'm now number one in the wedge. The guy on the cell phone is finally speaking to someone on the phone. The customer next to him looks comatose. The wedge behind me is longer and wider than when I first arrived. The number of people working the floor has varied from three to six, depending on the time, breaks, and when this guy ever gets off the phone, which by some miracle of thought, or prayer, or divine intervention, he does. It's a race between this guy filling out paperwork for the comatose customer and the woman filling out paperwork for the lady who has changed her mind three times over which phone to buy, to see who will draw me. Amazingly, it's the guy.

"Bonjour, Monsieur," I say.

"Bonjour, Monsieur," he says.

"J'ai une problem."

"Ouiiiii . . ." Already he senses trouble.

"L'année dernière je retour le Livebox ici. . . ." Last year I return the Livebox here, and I show him the papers with the signed, initialed, and stamped received notice, proving they have the Livebox, and I don't.

"Ouiiiiiii . . ." We're both holding the papers, neither of us willing to let go.

"Mais en novembre je recevoir une facture pour le Livebox, et le banc payee le facture pour quatre mois apres." But in

November I receive a bill for the Livebox, and the bank pay the bill for four months after, and I show him the bill from Orange and the automatic deductions taken from my account.

"Ouiiiiiiii . . ."

Then I say the hopefully magic words, "Je voudrais le reimbursement."

"Oui."

Is he kidding? Is it really going to be this simple? He turns to his computer, taps in my former internet account number, Livebox number, phone number, and maybe my IQ or DNA code, and in seconds confirms, Yes, I returned the Livebox, and, yes, they continued to bill me, and, yes, they owe me a refund. Holy cow! He picks up his phone and automatically calls a number his phone knows by heart, the same number he must have dialed for the comatose customer before me. I remember Eric when he set me up with the Livebox, and how he had to wait on the phone more than twenty minutes to get someone at Orange to help him—and this is worse.

I'm at Orange. This guy works for Orange—and he's calling the same number Eric called. There is no inside line, no direct line for employees working with customers in the Orange store. All calls from everyone—an employee in Quimper or someone from Vladivostok—go through the same number. I know, because after fifteen minutes, I ask: "Monsieur, avez-vous une numéro direct?"

He glares at me.

I guess not, and from what I can hear, which I can, because he placed the phone on speaker, there's no "Your call is very important to us." I don't know if that's better or worse than in the U.S, though it's certainly more honest.

Ten minutes more and someone answers. He explains the situation to the person on the other end, writes something down, and disconnects. He enters that something into the computer, turns to me, and says, "Bon. C'est fini."

"J'ai une reimbursement?"

"Oui."

"Quand?" When?

He shrugs.

It took two hours, but I have confirmation that I returned the Livebox and a promise of reimbursement sometime in the unknown future. What I don't have is this year's internet connection that I promised Donna I'd get. All I know is I'm never doing this again.

The next day I drive to Loscoat to see Eric, but he isn't there. Manu, the Buddha-faced guy, is. I know this immediately because when he sees me, computer and power cord with adapter plug in hand, his Buddha face falters, and he looks longingly at the back door, which is closed.

"Bonjour," I say.

"Bonjour, Marc."

I ask him about the past year, his life, family, the business—its third year of operation—the weather, everything I can think of and know how to say, to put him at ease, all of which makes him more edgy. Like who is this guy and why does he want to know all these things about me? Finally, I explain why I'm there, and as I do, his Buddha-face returns to normal: *this* is something he understands.

"L'année dernière je loue le Livebox et tout marche bien. Cette année je prefer achete une modem." Last year I rent the Livebox and all work well. This year I prefer buy a modem. Instead of keeping it for the summer only, I'll keep it year-round.

It's 25 euros a month, between four and five hundred dollars a year, but I won't have to change my password every year, and I'll never have to go back to Orange. Ever!

Manu recommends I buy a Netgear modem, which I do. He recommends it by taking it from the shelf and putting it in my hand. Then, either because Eric told him or he can plainly see for himself that I don't know anything, he downloads the software, sets up the computer and modem, and large-prints the new password clearly and simply, purposely *not* using French curlicue script so I can read it without my glasses. He even calls the phone company, waits the requisite twenty minutes—which is five minutes faster than for the poor guy in the Orange store—and authorizes Orange to begin internet service at my house.

As with Eric the previous year, Manu shows me where to plug the phone line and power line into the modem—and he plugs the power line into the slot in the modem right there, figuring it's one less possible problem for him to deal with. Unlike the previous year, he shows me four almost invisible icons on the modem and writes down their function: power; Wi-Fi; line; internet. All four lights need to be green. If power or Wi-Fi is red the problem is the modem. If line or internet is red the problem is the telephone. All of this is done with minimal conversation.

When he's finished, he charges me for the modem and sends me home, telling me the line will be connected in three or four days. I spent ninety minutes with him, where he downloaded the software and set everything up, including the twenty-minute call to Orange, and he didn't charge me anything for his time. It's a business model I wish they used in the U.S.

I drive back to the house, thrilled. I've got a refund—or a promise of a refund—from Orange and set up the internet so I'll never have to set it up again. *Last Time* has become one of the mantras of my life—last bed, roof replacement, car, paint job. . . . *Some* times, Last Time is inexplicably comforting.

I plug in the modem as Manu explained. The power cord is already in place, so that's easy. I plug the phone into the modem and watch as slowly, miraculously, one after the other, the four lights on the modem turn green, until the third one—line—flickers and turns red.

Manu said three or four days, so I wait.

On the seventh day, I explain to Manu that the line light was still red, which means there's a problem with the telephone, which brings me back to Orange. Manu asks me lots of questions, none of which I'd understand in English. Finally, in frustration or pity or hope for a better life, he says, "Je voudrais un rendez-vous chez vous aujourd'hui, cet après-midi." Holy cow! He's coming to my house after lunch.

In the U.S., the only doctor who still makes house calls is the coroner. Here the computer guy does. In the U.S., I can't even get the refrigerator fix-it guy I've hired and will pay beaucoup dollars to show up on the day and time he swears he will. Here, the sales guy—the guy from Best Buy, who sold me my computer system—drops by my house to see how I'm doing. Only I didn't even buy a system from Manu. I bought a modem for less than $100. Something is not working—is red—and Manu is coming to my house, probably not after his lunch, but cutting it short.

Sure enough, at 1:35, he knocks on the door.

"Entrez, entrez," I say, either telling him to enter or we're about to eat. "Une boisson," I ask—a drink?—probably complicating things.

He declines food and drink and asks to see the modem. "Le modem?"

I lead him to the TV/sitting room and show him the three glowing green lights and the flashing red.

"Votre ordinateur?"

I lead him up the stairs to my second-floor study and show him the computer. He turns it on, and takes out his phone . . . Merde . . . This time, though, it only takes him ten minutes to get through to Orange. I don't know what he says or does, but while he's on the phone, the icon on the computer screen with a giant red X on it disappears. I run down the stairs and see the red light is gone, and four bright, beaming, glowing green lights are blinking at me.

I run back up the stairs to tell Manu, but he already knows. I thank him profusely, "Merci, merci, merci beaucoup," and I offer to pay him for his time and expertise. "Combien pour tout, pour tout le travail?"

"Non, non, normal," he says, and gets out of there before anything else can go wrong. But nothing does.

A week later I give him a bottle of twelve-year-old Wild Turkey and thank him again profusely, "Merci, merci beaucoup." And every time I pass the store, I do the same. I wave and call, "Bonjour," and add with a smile, "Tout est marche bien." All is work well. I buy all my computer supplies from Eric and Manu even though they are slightly more expensive than the chain stores. For their sake and mine, I want these guys around.

Two weeks later, I'm back at the Orange store in Quimper. Madame P wants to return the phone I bought for her *last* year. God knows how she is going to do this, but I know she will. She wants me to go with her to (1) verify I bought the phone there, though the receipt clearly shows that, and (2) to help her select a new one, which, since I selected the wrong one the first time, seems odd to me.

We enter the wedge and wait. While we're waiting, the guy who helped me with the refund sees me and falters. Actually, literally. He doesn't even have the heart to hide it. To put him at ease, I walk over to him and say, "Pas moi," not me. "Je suis ici avec mon amie," I am here with my friend, and point to Madame P.

"Bon," he says. "Merci."

Little does he know that in an hour or two, he's going to wish he was dealing with me. I might be incomprehensible, but I'm a pushover, as I have zero ability to retort, question, or respond, and I don't know the rules or my rights, but Yvonne does, and by the time we leave the store with her new phone—which he discounted twice—he never, ever wants to see either of us again.

We cross the cathedral square and sit at a café facing the side of the cathedral and eat ice cream. She has a new phone she knows how to use, and I have the internet. It doesn't get much better than that. Unfortunately, that's the truth, but here's the strangest thing: I have a massive sense of accomplishment. It's one of the things I like most about living in France. In the U.S., I give up or ask Bob or pay someone. In France, I do it myself—or try to. In the U.S., I get frustrated and angry that things don't work as I want, or as I think they should, and my blood pressure goes up and probably takes years off my life. In France, my sense of accomplishment increases my sense of well-being and hopefully, I want to think, adds time.

II

I intend to live forever. So far, so good.
—Steven Wright

Knock, Knock

In the U.S., hardly anyone knocks on our door unannounced, and I prefer it that way. In Plobien, everyone does, and I prefer it that way, too.

The electric meter guy from EDF knocks, usually within a day or two of my arrival. I have no idea how he knows I'm there. The dehumidifier is on 24/7 twelve months a year, so the electricity is always on. The knock is a loud, repeated, we-mean-business knock, though the person knocking is always a young lad, clipboard in hand, kind of sheepish or shy. I know he's the electric guy by the clipboard in his hand and the speed with which he speaks. Basically, he just wants to get me over with. Newer houses, as almost all houses in the U.S, have their meters outside and are read either electronically, by computer, or on-site, without needing entry to the home. My house, though, is older, almost 150 years old now, and the meter is inside, above the refrigerator. I've inquired about getting a new meter and placing it outside, but the cost is prohibitive—and they won't place it where I want. The front wall of my house is a gorgeous rust, blue, black, and gray tweed of slate and granite.

I want the meter on the side of the house, out of sight. To me it's a matter of aesthetics, something I'd expect French people to care about. To EDF, it's illogical. The meter should be easily accessible and visible and should have the shortest, fastest, easiest—all of which means cheapest—connection. So my meter is still in the house, and every year a new, seemingly younger (because I'm older) meter guy knocks on the door.

"Bonjour," I say, wait for him to say whatever he says, and show him in. I open the cabinet door that hides the meter. He reads the meter and writes the numbers down. "Merci," he thanks me. "Merci beaucoup," I thank him, and he leaves. A month later, I receive a bill and a notice from EDF. The bill tells me how much I owe them or they owe me (which has never happened) for the previous twelve months, and the notice tells me what I will owe them for the next twelve months, and how much they will automatically deduct from my bank account each month now that I've finally set up an automatic deduction.

The water meter guy also knocks, probably a lot, because he comes in winter when nobody's here. When I arrive in summer, there's a card waiting for me with directions on how to read the meter and fill out the card. It's all very clear and simple—and impossible. My water meter, like my electric meter, is inside the house. Unlike the electric meter, it's impossible to read. First, it's on the floor, under the sink, which means I have to crawl into the cabinet with all the cleaning supplies and solvents to find it. Second, it's dark, so I need a flashlight. Third, the floor is cold and often damp, and I have to lie on it to read the meter, which no matter what I do, I can't, because it is upside down. I don't know why, but it is. And even when I've had it replaced, it remains upside down. But that's not the real challenge. I can read the upside-down numbers with a mirror:

mirror in one hand, pen in the other, flashlight in my mouth, pad on the floor, I'm ready to write the numbers—except for the water. The face of the meter is blurred by water. Not on the outside, but inside, making the meter impossible to read, which means every summer I have to go to the water company and make an appointment to have the meter read.

First, I have to find the water company, as the office changes locations every few years. Second, I have to find it open, as the hours are odd, and they too have changed over the years: say, closed Monday, open Tuesday, 10:00–12:00, closed Wednesday, open Thursday 1:30–4:30, Fridays maybe, Saturdays, theoretically. This requires multiple visits, as the office is often closed the hours it's supposed to be open and open when it's supposed to be closed. Still, eventually, mostly by luck, I do find it and find it open and manage to explain that I want to fill out their card and save them a trip, but I can't read the meter. It goes like this:

"Bonjour, Madame . . ." The person I'm speaking with looks sixteen, but there's no way I'm calling her mademoiselle... I hand her the blank water meter reader card, and say, "Cette carte est très bien, mais c'est ne pas possible lire le metre parceque beaucoup d'eau dans l'interior le metre." This card is very good, but it is not possible to read the yardstick because a lot of water in the interior the yardstick. Metre it turns out means meter, as in one meter long. Water meter is compteur d'eau.

She takes the blank card, starts to say something, and stops. It's clear she doesn't know if she should believe what she just heard—or even if she just heard what she thinks she heard. I stand there and wait, and eventually she does what I need. She opens the giant ledger on her desk, checks her computer, and we make an appointment—usually weeks in the future—for the water meter person to visit the house. It takes so long, apparently, because water meter reading seems to be a winter activity, and it's summer now, and the meter reader person works stranger hours than when the office is open.

We do get there, though, and on the appointed day, almost at the appointed hour, there's a knock on the door. "Bonjour," I say, shake the guy's hand, and lead him into the kitchen, where the under-the-sink cabinet doors are open, and the cleaning supplies and solvents are all pushed to one corner. He looks at me like, "merde."

He's big and the space is small. It's also, he knows, cold and probably wet. He's wearing nice pants, nice shirt, good shoes. This wasn't what he expected. He crawls into the cabinet, flashlight and pad in hands, ready to finish and get out of there as fast as he can, and he can't: the numbers are upside down and there's water in the meter. He looks at me like, "double merde."

I hand him a mirror, and he says, "Merci." After a few minutes of fumbling around and muttering, I hand him a plumber's wrench, and he says, "Merci." He then turns the water off, removes the meter, shakes out the water, and reads it. Years ago, probably in hope of never having to do this again—or helping the next guy, as the same person never appears twice—the guy went to his van and returned with a new meter. I thanked him profusely, but when I went to read it the following year the numbers were upside down and impossible to read because water blurred the face. I've asked about placing the meter outside, where it would be more accessible to read, but Madame/Mademoiselle said it would cost too much, and they didn't really want to do it. Apparently, they'd rather send someone in winter, when no one is at the house, and set up a special appointment to send someone to the house to read the meter in summer. All I can figure is this is another way of providing employment. A few days after the meter reader's visit, I receive a bill and a notice from the water company, telling me what I owe them or they owe me (which has never happened) for the previous twelve months, and what they'll automatically deduct from my bank account for the next twelve months.

The post person knocks when s/he can't fit the mail through the slot in the door. Actually, I'm amazed s/he even tries, as I'm the only person in the village with a stand-alone unattached house and a mail slot in my door. Everyone else has a mailbox at the side of the road. The mail person drives down the road, stops at the right house—even though most houses have no number—and delivers the mail. At my house, the post person has to stop the van, get out, walk down my driveway— about seventy-five feet—often in the rain, as it's Brittany, and try to fit the mail through the slot. I know I should put a mail-box on the post next to the road for the mail person, but I'm too American and worried about theft, especially identity theft, to do it, even though I can't imagine who in this village or France would want to be me.

The post person also knocks on my door whenever there is a letter or parcel addressed to a person or place s/he doesn't know, or a handwriting s/he can't read. I've become the dead letter box in Plobien, as in, "If we don't know where it goes, it must be for him." Often enough, it is.

Twice in the past thirty years, my neighbors have knocked on my door unannounced. The first time was the first summer I was here when Georges, my then neighbor to the west—a trim, middle-aged, silver-haired fellow in pressed pants, polished shoes, a crisp shirt and mustache, and his pretty, flowery-dressed, English-speaking adult daughter, Catherine, knocked on my door. I knew it wasn't a social visit—not the French Welcome Wagon—from their obvious discomfort and refusal of a drink. They were there to deliver unwanted news, I knew that. What I didn't know was what it was. Then they told me: my trees are too brown on their side and too tall; they're ugly and blocking the sun, keeping it from their garden, and they told me their rights: in France, if your neighbor's trees— *My* trees!—are within two meters (six feet) of your property— *Their* property!—and more than two meters tall, they have the right to have the neighbor— *Me!*—cut the trees to two meters height. I balked. I stammered. I loved those trees— thirty cypress trees, twenty-five to thirty feet tall, separating my house from theirs, providing privacy, which apparently I cared about more than they. I promised to trim the trees, clean out the dead branches and needles, do anything they wanted, except cut them. We discussed it for an hour, and they left.

The following fall, I had the trees trimmed and cleaned, and when I returned in the summer nothing more was said. Nothing more was ever said until years later when Georges's brother-in-law, my now neighbor François, bought the house from his sister and moved in permanently.

The second time a neighbor knocked on my door unannounced was a few years ago. I was watching TV and heard a knock on the door. I opened it and a very attractive, short, bronzed, golden-haired woman, who smelled like gardenias, dressed all in white, was standing in my doorway, smiling. I didn't know if I should be happy about this or not. "Je m'appelle Françoise," she said, and explained—several times, in *very* slow French—that she's my new neighbor and wants to thank me for the bottle of wine I'd totally forgotten about.

The previous year, the day before Donna and I returned to California, I made a willful effort to be a good neighbor (something I have never done with any neighbor, new or old, in the U.S.) and went next door and handed the fellow who'd been working on the house for the past three weeks a bottle of good Bordeaux, saying, "Pour bienvenue le nouveau propriétaire." For welcome the new owner. "J'habite à côté." I live beside.

Now, the new neighbor is here. "Je suis Mark," I say, and hold out my hand to shake. She shakes it, and says, "Nous aimerions vous inviter pour l'apéritif ce soir," and happy as I am to have friendly new neighbors, I panic: apéritif means a couple of hours of nibbling and drinking and speaking French, two of the three at which I excel. I demur. She insists, and I follow her next door to meet her husband, Bruno, who thankfully is bilingual French-English—and the first of hundreds of knocks begin.

People from the *Mairie* used to knock on my door every July to collect money for the Fête Nautique, but that ended years ago when they stopped the fête for lack of funds. Now, they knock to hand me the village newsletter. If I'm not home, they push it through the slot in the door.

Once, when the village of Loscoat wanted to build a water filtration plant across the river in our part of Plobien—the Wild West, the boonies—someone knocked on my door and asked me to sign a petition opposing it. I happily did, though I couldn't read it or understand much of what the person distributing the petition said. I think she was relieved I could sign my name and didn't write an X—or whatever French people use to verify illiteracy.

Friends, like Jean-Pierre and Jöelle, ride their bikes along the old canal towpath that's across the road from the house and stop to knock on the door to say "Bonjour." Sometimes, if I beg and plead long and hard enough, they'll come in for a drink of water, which is all they will ever take. Hugo, the fellow who refinished all the floors in the house, knocks on the door if he sees my car in the driveway. He gives me a big California guy-to-guy bear hug and invites me to dinner later in the summer when Donna is here. Monsieur C, my plumber-friend, periodically comes by to check on the furnace and make sure it's still working. Sometimes he knocks and comes in for a cup of coffee. Other times, he just checks the furnace and leaves.

Madame P knocks when she arrives to work in her garden, which is at my house because I have more land than she. She knocks often—sometimes twice a day, depending on heat, drought, sun, rain, wind, and whim.

I always invite her in when she knocks. I give her four cheek kisses, and say "Entrez s'il vous plait" when she arrives and offer her a drink. "Une boisson? Une verre de l'eau, jus, du thé?" A glass of water, juice, or tea, as I know that's all she will drink. She never says "Oui," only "Apres," *after* she's worked in the garden, as if she doesn't deserve it yet. I do the same when she leaves. I say "Entrez s'il vous plait" and offer her "Une boisson?" but unless it is unseasonably hot, which more and more it is, or she has something particularly newsy to tell me, she declines, pointing to her earthy hands and espadrilles, but thinking, I think, she'll disturb me and interfere with something important, like my afternoon nap or writing about her and her family.

Sharon is the only person who regularly knocks in the morning. Sometimes she calls first and asks if I'm writing, ostensibly so as not to interrupt, but probably wondering if I'm writing about her and Jean. I know this because years ago when

Jean fixed my dehumidifier, making it better and stronger than when it was new, he asked, "Is this going to be in your next book?"

"It is now," I said, once again confirming the Heisenberg effect.

She stops for a chat, cigarette, and cup of coffee on her way to or from shopping in Loscoat. She knocks on the door and calls, "Mark." I stop what I'm doing when I hear her and run down the stairs, holding on to the banister—something I began doing a few years ago—and greet her with a hearty "Bonjour" and four cheek kisses. I know she thinks this is excessive because she returns one or two, letting me know that's enough—but until she tells me to stop, or I see her wiping a kiss or two away, I'll continue. I've known her for thirty years now, just a few days fewer than I've known Madame P.

She always sits on the chair facing the fireplace in the dining room, her back to the yard and kitchen window. I hand her an ashtray—something she and I both know I wouldn't do if Donna was here. When Donna's here, everyone smokes outside no matter the weather: the worse the weather, the happier Donna is, thinking/hoping it will dissuade them, though, of course, it never does.

I put a can of *lait concentré*—evaporated milk—on the table for me, because I always put milk in my coffee, but if it's after ten o'clock in the morning, it's a no-no in France—and identifies me as a Philistine or an American, which in France are about the same. I fill our cups—hers halfway, because that's all she ever wants, and mine to the top, allowing room for milk—and we talk about the latest Booker Prize winner and the Goncourt, *Charlie Hebdo*, who is the worst leader—Macron, Trump, or Le Pen—and *Le Canard Enchainé* (The Chained

Duck, a magazine like *The Onion*), which I wish I could read and understand, but can't, and the latest *New Yorker*, which she and Jean do read and are more up-to-date on than I am. The only thing they don't understand is the occasional cartoon or cover. Sometimes I can help them, and sometimes not. What bothers them most are the ads for expensive, luxurious polluting products when the magazine hypocritically presents itself as a fighter for the environment—and grammar: the umlaut over the o and e in coöperate and preëmptive, the lack of the subjective tense, and the illogical way Americans use quotation marks, different from the English, French, and Australians.

Strangers knock on my door. One night, after midnight, I heard a loud banging on the door. I got out of bed, put on my pants, ran down the stairs, and opened the door—something I would never do in the middle of the night in the U.S.

Standing in front of me was a huge, red-faced—and this is in the dark—bearded, very distraught fellow, speaking worse French than mine.

"English?" I ask.

"Oh, yes. You're the American? My boat is stuck in the mud, I can't find the lockkeeper, and I'm afraid the keel may break."

I don't know anything about boats, but I've lived on the canal, which at this point is tidal, long enough to know this: "There's nothing you can do except stabilize the boat, secure it, and wait five or six hours for the tide." Then, to my utter amazement, I invite him to spend the night, but he's too worried about his boat, and declines. The next day, when I return from the beach, I find a bottle of Johnny Walker Blue and a note saying "Thanks, mate" in front of my door.

After my book *I'll Never Be French (no matter what I do)* was published as *Jamais Je Ne Serai Français* (*Never Will I Be*

French) in French and *Nie bede Francuzem* in Polish, I received hundreds of emails, dozens of letters, a score of phone calls, and several unannounced visitors knocking on my door. Thankfully, luckily, *amazingly*, most of the local people who read the book enjoy it and stop me on the street or in the *super-marché* to tell me. So I'm not worried about being punched in the nose—or worse, shot—when I hear a knock, open the door, and see four middle-aged people, two men and two women, standing in the doorway, two of them giggling. Unless they're diabolical, which they don't seem to be—but who can really tell?—they seem okay.

"Monsieur Greenside?" The fellow in front holds out his hand to shake. The woman next to him clutches a bottle of wine.

"Oui." I shake his hand.

"Jean-Yves," he says, and points to the woman. "Catherine." Then he points to the giggling people behind him. "Lauren and Tom."

I shake everyone's hand, and we stand there, me trying to decide if I should invite them in, them trying to decide if they made a mistake.

"I write to you by internet," says Jean-Yves.

Thank God, he speaks English.

"I read your book . . ."

"Oh! Yes, Jean-Yves and Catherine." I don't have a clue.

He tells me he wrote and told me they live in the southeast, near Lyon, but he went to school in Brittany, and he identified the real name of Plobien and where, exactly, I live. I remember I wasn't very happy when I read that. I wrote the book to be read, not found—and now here he is with his wife and their friends. "You said if I ever come back I should visit you for a drink."

In the U.S., when you say this—like "later," or "I'll call you," or "let's do lunch"—it means goodbye. In France, apparently, it means hello. "Entrez, entrez," I say, always braver and more forthcoming with my French when I'm speaking with someone who speaks English.

I lead them to the terrace, and we spend the rest of the afternoon exchanging stories, nibbling on Madame P's still warm-from-the-earth baby radishes, dipping them in Breton fleur-de-sel butter. We drink Catherine's delicious, fruity Macon-Villages chardonnay, straight from her sister's vineyard, eat meats from the local charcuterie, open a bottle of Haut Médoc, and finish with fresh strawberries from Plougastel for dessert.

They leave three hours later, all of us happy, smiling, laughing, sated, drunk. Jean-Yves and Catherine invite me to visit them in southeastern France, which, since they're French, and French people never make these offers unless they mean it, I plan to do. Tom and Lauren also invite me to visit them, in Ashland, Oregon, but since they're American I dismiss it as "let's do lunch," until they repeat it several times, each time with greater and greater emphasis, and reiterate it, in writing, in two notes. Now, I think the invitations might be real and plan to take them up on it.

Even Jehovah's Witnesses knock, and politely, immediately leave when I say, "Je suis Juif." I'm Jewish.

In the U.S., "knock, knock" is the beginning of a joke. In France, it's the beginning of the most important thing in French life, more important than food, wine, sex, or sport: it's the start of a conversation.

"Hello. It's me. I'm here . . ."

A Gift to You

When *I'll Never Be French (no matter what I do)* was published I decided to give a copy to each of the French people in the book, even if they couldn't read it—*especially* if they couldn't read it, because I didn't want them to learn about the book from someone else, and worry what it said about them.

I was so certain of my motives and good intentions—to write a paean and thank-you, a love letter to Plobien, Brittany, France, and the people who helped me—I couldn't imagine anything going wrong, which is odd, actually, considering the book chronicles everything I don't know about Brittany, France, and French people. Given the magnitude of my ignorance, the magnitude of my surety was astounding. Basically, I was counting on my goodwill and intent—and the fact that most of the French people I know can't read English.

Still, I didn't want to lose any friends, and I didn't want to have to move, so I followed George W. Bush's well-thought-out Gulf War II plan and fired a preemptive shot, hoping for better results than he got.

I met with the oil guy's son, the floor guy, the *Notaire,* the restaurant owners who hosted my fiftieth birthday, my neighbor François, Monsieur Charles, Madame P, and the insurance guy, and gave each person a signed copy, saying, "C'est une cadeau pour tout vous avez donné moi." It's a gift for all you have give me—and I hoped if they were offended by anything I wrote, they would know it was not intentional and forgive me.

The reaction was universal surprise for the gift, and amazement that I, a functional illiterate in France, could write anything. I pointed to my name on the book jacket to prove it, and said, "J'ai ecrire cette livre, parce que j'aime beaucoup mon vie en France." I have write this book because I love my life in France."

They looked at me as if I was giving them porn.

Once they got over their shock, I showed them where I'd written about them. Given my French, who knows what I actually said or what they heard, but everyone laughed, and no one seemed angry or upset. The only person I worried about was Monsieur Claude, the insurance guy, who I didn't know as well as the others. I was anxious about how I portrayed him, especially with all his blinking and squinting. To American eyes, I know he appears kind, sympathetic, and funny, but to French eyes—*his* eyes—I hadn't a clue.

I waited until the week before the return flight to California to meet with him in case I had to get out of town in a hurry. I entered his office, as usual, without an appointment, and handed him a copy of the book. Like everyone else, he was surprised that I could write anything. I showed him where I'd signed the book to him and pointed out the chapter with the insurance questions I'd asked him. He seemed happy, and I was too, and relieved, until he shook my hand and said "Merci," and added, "My wife she reads English very well."

"Bon," I said. "Bien. L'année prochaine." Good. Good. See you next year, and I hoped time and distance would temper his and her response if it was negative.

All in all, I thought I'd done okay. I hadn't made any new enemies and didn't make a fool of myself—at least as far as I knew.

That night at dinner at Jean and Sharon's I told Donna and them what I'd been doing and saying, proudly concluding with, "J'aime beaucoup mon vie en France."

This is when Jean told me about *mon vie*. He shook his head in dismay or disgust or disbelief, maybe all three, and said, "Marc, do you know what you're saying? You love your dick. You love your dick in France. *Mon* vie is your dick. *Ma* vie is your life." All the while, he was pointing to his crotch, repeating, "Mon vie, mon vie . . ."

No wonder people looked at me as if I was handing them porn.

The next several months I worried about the insurance guy and his English reading wife's lengthening silence. If good news travels fast, this can only be terrible. At Christmas time, I received a card from them. The handwriting was more American than French, so I knew it was from her. I opened the envelope with trepidation, hoping it wasn't a subpoena and I didn't need to find a new insurance agent, and read, in perfect English, that they enjoyed the book, laughed a lot, and gave copies to their family and friends as holiday gifts. It was the best present they could have given me, a triple A gift: Appreciation, Approval, and Acceptance. Talk about enhancing life! I couldn't ask for anything more.

Then there's this . . .

I'm Pollutante (Polluting)

In October, I received an official-looking letter on letterhead stationery from something called SPANC—Service Public d'Assainissement Non Collectif. I have no idea who they are or what they want, but I'm not too concerned, as I often get official-looking letters that say a lot and mean nothing. In the U.S., they're mostly from my bank and my insurance company, telling me about my nonexistent privacy rights and why my rates are going up for the fewer and poorer services they still provide. I get the letters, don't read them, and toss them, which is probably what they're counting on. In France, though, I read them and try to figure out what they mean, and when I can't, which is most of the time, I ask my bilingual friends—Sharon, Jean, Bruno, or Gilles—if I need to do anything, and they read them and toss them. This letter, though, looks important. It's entitled Diagnostic Assainissement Avis de Passage # 1. The key word is *assainissement*.

"Donna," I call from the living room, "do you know what *assainissement* means?"

"No," she calls back from her office, where she's working—and that's that. This is our arrangement: the California house is (mostly) her responsibility, the French house is (mostly) mine.

I look up *assainir*, to clean up. It's something about cleaning up passage #1, whatever that is, and I hope there aren't any passages #2, 3, or 4. I haven't a clue, but it doesn't bode well. The letter proposes a rendezvous at the house in Plobien on Tuesday, November 17, the same day I have a colonoscopy exam in California. Guess where I'd rather be?

I email Bruno and Françoise, my unlucky-for-them, lucky-for-me next-door neighbors. "Did you get the *assainissement* letter? What does it mean?"

"Yes, we have one also," Bruno writes. "It's about sewers."

"Merde."

"Exactly."

Once again, it seems Plobien is attempting to complete its sewer line. Twenty years ago, it completed the line for half the village, for everyone living east of the *Mairie*, then ran out of money. Ten years ago, they dug west another 25 percent and ran out of money. Now, they are planning to complete the last quadrant and dig a sewer line in the wild, wild west of Plobien, Kostez Gwer, the green side, where I live.

Of course, I support this. What's not to support? Sewer lines are safer, cleaner, and more efficient than septic tanks, though I've had no troubles with mine for almost twenty-five years. The issue isn't the principle, it's the principal, which I don't have, especially if I also need to replace my furnace, which, according to Monsieur C, my ever-ready, reliable plumber-friend, I do. It works like this: the village uses local and national funds—tax money, *my* money—to dig the ditch, lay the pipe, and fill the ditch that runs along the main road.

Then *I* use my money to dig the ditch, lay the pipe, and fill the ditch that connects my house to the main line, which people who live on the sewer side of town tell me cost about 7,000 euros, about $7,500, *ten* years ago, *if* there are no problems, which in an older house like mine, there always are.

I write back to SPANC, "J'habit dans les Étas Unis. La maison en Plobien est une maison secondaire. C'est fermé pour hiver," and I propose a rendezvous in late June.

This is how I learn the word propose is not a suggestion in French. They write back, "November 17. Be there!"

I call Bruno and Françoise. "Do *you* have to be at your house on November 17—a Tuesday?" I'm convinced this is some new National Front let's-get-the-foreigners-out-of-here movement. Tuesday is a working day for Bruno, a working day in another village two hours away, as theirs is a *maison secondaire* also. No way will he have to be there.

"Yes, of course."

"Really?"

"Bien-sûr."

"What do *I* do? I can't be there."

"Don't worry. I'll take care of it. Do you know where your septic tank is?"

I've lived more than seven decades and no one has ever asked me that question. Why should they? Everything has always worked fine. I've had no troubles, questions, or curiosity, only the occasional fear that the tank would break or leak or clog—or whatever it does when it doesn't work—and this day would come. "I think if you face the house, it's somewhere to the left, in front of the bushes . . ." which is why, I just realized, everything planted there thrives.

"Okay. Don't worry. I'll find it."

Bruno is six-foot-three, weighs almost two hundred pounds—a giant in France—how hard can this be? On November 18, Françoise shows me. She emails me photos of Bruno streaked with what I hope to heaven is mud. He's fifty years old, an oncologist, and he's digging a hole—lots of holes—in my front yard—in the rain. There are photos of him bare-chested, wearing his funky plaid summer shorts and flip-flops, brown holes—a moonscape—all around him, as he digs and searches for the cover of my septic tank. There are photos of him sopping wet, hair dripping, getting progressively browner, as he locates the Eureka! Voilà! Honeypot. There are photos of him prying open and lifting the twenty-five-kilo, fifty-five-pound cement lid, and attaching a forty-euro, fifty-dollar strap that he bought, so the next time he does this, because he knows there will be a next time, it won't be so difficult and he won't be so brown. Finally, there are photos of him closing the lid after the inspection—whatever they looked at or for—and covering the lid with dirt.

For Bruno, my neighbor, my friend, it's a day in the country. For me, it's a miracle: he drives two hours to get there and another two to get home; he digs up the yard at his house, and then he comes next door and digs up mine. In the rain! In the U.S., the only person who would do this is a hungry, undocumented immigrant begging for work no citizen would do, or the undertaker.

"Merci, merci beaucoup," I write back. "How did it go?"

"No problem. There are no leaks. Now, we wait for the report."

"What report?"

"I don't know. We wait," something he and all other French people are much better at than I. I want my chores and busyness over with as quickly as possible so I can get on with living my life, because I still haven't accepted this is my life.

Three months later, I receive a package from SPANC. I open it and find a letter and a ten-page, small-print report complete with photos of my septic tank, washing machine discharge hose, and kitchen degreaser, something I didn't even know existed until it clogged, overflowed, and stank like rot before Monsieur C fixed it. The one word in the cover letter that I do understand is: *pollutante*, polluting.

My first thought is I hope the Sierra Club and Greenpeace don't find out. Then what I feel is chagrin. I love this land and my house and my life here, the fresh mussels and oysters and heather-covered hills, unsoiled beaches, and opal to turquoise seas. The last thing I want to do is to add to the gazillion tons of nitrates from the pig shit that farmers spray over the land as fertilizer, ruining the air, sea, and ground water. Compared to them, my pollutants are nothing. Added to them, my pollutants are everything. If political change begins at home, I'm a royalist . . .

I use a green, eco-friendly, nature-pure laundry detergent called OMO—Old Mother Owl! Go figure—and the plants around the shed, where my washing machine lives, are happy. White lilies, yellow and red roses, blue and white hydrangeas, all bloom brilliantly, stand proudly, none drooping or complaining about the rinse cycle that feeds them all summer. Still, the machine *is* discharging dirty water onto the land, where it seeps into the ground, and runs into the river and sea—and green, eco-friendly, nature-pure OMO probably is not clean enough. The kitchen degreaser, a tripart purifier system that separates fats from water, has been here forever, though. *Every* old house has one. What's the need to change it? What's the rush?

I email Bruno. "Je suis pollutante, et vous?"

"Oui. Tout le monde est polluant. C'est obligatoire les égouts" (a word I know from World War II, the French Résistance, and a tour of the Paris sewers). Everyone is polluting. Sewers are mandatory.

"What about the report? What else does it say in ten pages of small print?"

Bruno explains the report has three parts. First, it documents and proves I'm pollutante: tout le monde est polluants. Second, it provides a list of certified and approved business enterprises to do the work to make me non-pollutante. The longest and densest part explains their authority and power and the SPANCing I will get if I don't do what they want.

"What do they want? What do I have to do?"

"Nothing."

"Nothing?"

"First, the village has to dig the sewer line."

"When will that happen?"

"It doesn't say."

France is in the midst of another recession. There is no easily available money, and as much as I want and believe in sewer lines, I'm relieved. The shed, where the washing machine resides, is to the east, the non-septic tank side of the house, at least 120 feet from the septic tank, where the new sewer line from the house to the main would be. The kitchen degreaser is to the west of the septic tank side of the house, at least thirty feet from the septic tank and the new sewer line to the main. If the one sewer line from the house to the main—about seventy feet—without any problems cost $7,500 ten years ago, two other sewer lines and another 150 feet of no-problem digging and laying of pipe would double that, and with complications, maybe triple it.

"Is that it?"

"No. You owe them eighty-five euros for the report."

I send a check to SPANC for eighty-five euros and a check to Bruno for 220 euros, forty for the strap he bought so he could find and easily lift the septic tank cover the next time he has to do this—something we both know will happen, though hopefully not soon—and 180 euros for the company he hired to clean the septic tank, the first time in twenty-five years. That's that, I hope, thinking any new sewer line is years, maybe decades away.

Two months later I receive a letter from the mayor of Plobien telling me he received a copy of the report identifying me as *pollutante*, and he and the village will come up with a plan by the end of the year.

Nine years later I get an email from Sharon. "They're digging up the road for the sewers!" She's Irish and Catholic, so she's comfortable giving bad news—but she doesn't live in Plobien. Maybe it's road repairs, I think, though the roads are perfect. Maybe it's another unneeded speed bump or *rond-point*.

I email Ella, who is English and Protestant *and* lives in Plobien. "Sharon said they've begun digging the sewer lines."

"Yes, they are, but we just sold our house and bought a place in Loscoat that's already connected."

"I'm happy for *you*," I write back, not bothering to tell her how *I* feel.

A few days later, a letter from the mayor arrives telling me work on the sewers is about to begin.

All winter, Ella and Sharon keep me apprised of the progress: "They began at the chartreuse house. . . . They're at the new chandlery. . . . The quay in front of the baker's house. . . . The viaduct. . . . Ella and Rick's former house. . . .

The park for campers across the street from my house where sheep now graze . . ."

I'm following their progress, hoping they finish before I arrive so I won't have to deal with the mud, noise, and traffic, when that worry is superseded by another: an article Sharon sends about the sewer system the village is installing—a new vacuum system, the first such system in the world. When I read this I immediately think of BART, the Bay Area (not-so) Rapid Transit System that gets slower and more unreliable every year.

The BART board, in its ignorance and arrogance, wanted a transit system that was new and different and unique, and that's exactly what they got: a system so unique that replacement parts no longer exist, and fifty years later lots of replacement parts are needed. To get them, they have to be fabricated, meaning the costs are outlandish, replacement takes a long time, and the system is constantly broke, money-wise and operationally. That's the bad news. The good news is Plobien's new vacuum sewer system is German, which gives me hope until I remember Volkswagen and what they did with the waste emissions from their cars, which leaves me with visions of backed-up sewage in the sink, on the floors, in the grout, the rugs, everyplace but the toilet. It's good to have imagination as a writer, but not so good for daily living and life.

They finish the work in May. I arrive in June, surprised that the road is fully repaired and paved and looks better than any road in the San Francisco Bay Area.

A few days later, I call Rick and Ella to set a time to visit their new, already sewer-connected home in Loscoat and pay them for the work they've done the previous nine months. I also want a sewer-connection referral from Rick. He's retiled my bathrooms, replumbed and built a new shower, built oak cabinets for the kitchen, laid out the stone driveway, and painted and repainted everything paintable in the house. He made the interior of his old, former house look California modern. At a friend's house, he designed, cut, and completely fabricated a new art deco marble bathroom. There is nothing he can't build and no material he can't work with, which is why he's my French Consumer Reports, Better Business Bureau, and Angi-guy all in one. Any product he says to buy, I buy. Any person he recommends for work, I hire. So, after setting the day and time for my visit, I ask him, "Who would you use to dig the ditch and connect to the mains if you had to do it at your house?"

"Monsieur N," he says, and I know who I'm going to call.

My plan is to get the work done quickly, before Monsieur N gets too busy and I wind up at the end of the line. Ha! No one in Plobien is in a hurry. No one wants to be first. They, being French—Breton—are programmed to wait, hold back, expect a change or delay, administrative blindness, ineptitude, collapse. I, being American, am programmed to be first and fastest, to get this over with and off my list: jump into the ice-cold water; rip that Band-Aid off; don't let the snow, rain, heat, or fog—anything—stop me. I call Monsieur N the next day.

"Bonjour, Monsieur. Monsieur Rick donne moi votre nom et numéro. C'est possible vous visitez chez moi pour le rendez-vous?" Rick gave me your name and number. Can you visit me for a rendezvous?

"Oui, bien sûr. Mardi prochain, après midi." Next Tuesday after lunch.

I hang up the phone elated, satisfied with a job well done, until I realize I never told him why I called. I hope he understands, and that he's not a member of some secret dating club, which is what rendezvous means to me.

He arrives on time, dressed like a worker, not like he's on a date, and I hand him a copy of the SPANC report and point to where the washing machine and kitchen degreaser are. He walks to each one, making notes, counting steps, walking frontward, backward, surveying all . . . All I can see are Euro signs. After ten minutes—which seems a very short time—he shakes my hand and says, in English, "I send you a devis"—a binding estimate—"by post."

Ten days later it arrives. I open the letter with trepidation. Holy cow! He's charging me 2,500 euros, about $3,000, 4,500 less than I expected to pay. I'm overjoyed, feeling rich, until I hear from my friend who heard from her friend who works in the *Mairie* that the village is planning to tax everyone an *additional* 2,500 euros to pay for the digging of the main sewer line.

I'm conflicted. On the one hand, 5,000 euros is about $2,000 less than I expected to pay. On the other hand, I *already* paid those additional 2,500 euros with my taxes, and when I find out later that the rest of the village—the people who hooked up ten and twenty years ago—didn't pay any additional fees, I want to pay them even less. That, plus my fears—now becoming a certainty—that the new, untried, Volkswagen sewer system won't work, the river will overflow again, and the resulting swell won't be so swell for me.

I email Bruno and ask what he knows about the additional 2,500-euro tax. "Nothing." I ask Mr. Charles, Mr. C, Madame P. No one knows anything. There's been no public announcement, no letter from the mayor or public treasury. How I—a functional illiterate—could know this before anyone else is astonishing. Then I remember the Maastricht Treaty, when

France joined the European Union. I asked people what they thought of the treaty, about specific provisions, about how their money would change, trade, food products, border controls, and no one knew anything. I knew more about Maastricht than they did, not that it mattered, because I couldn't vote. Nor, it turned out, could they. The French government approved the treaty—as maybe it did the sewer tax—with not much knowledge of the electorate. It's enough to make me reconsider libertarianism . . .

Seven months later I receive the bill from Monsieur N, telling me he has completed the work. Ted and Lynda are arriving, so I'll find out soon enough if he has, and how well it works. All I know for sure is I am one of two households in our part of Plobien—the other is probably a Brit—who are connected to the main sewer line. What I don't know is if this is good news or bad and whether it's better to be first or last.

I console myself with the thought that at least this part of my French life—my septic tank life—is over, and I won't have to worry about it breaking or leaking anymore.

Some people have a bucket list of things they want to do before they die. I have a bucket list of things I hope never happen, or never happen again, like a colonoscopy, CT scan, or kidney stones—and for the first time ever I wonder if Methuselah endured medical interventions, if he whined, worried, or complained, and if they added to his 969 years, or cut him short . . .

Bees in My Chimney, Again

In the U.S., time is linear, moving in one direction: forward. This used to mean progress, now it means there's an end. In France, time is circular: been there, done that, again and again, like circling a roundabout, buying the wrong mattress cover three times, and having bees in my chimney, again.

For the past two weeks Emily has been emailing me and monitoring their progress. She began with a few bees in the second floor bedroom. "There are bees in the bedroom," she wrote.

"Are you allergic?" I wrote back.

"No."

"Then don't worry." Like every other house and apartment in France, there are no screens on the windows or doors. Flies enter on the first floor, bees and sometimes birds on the second, and bats on the third. "It's warm, sunny, flowers are in bloom, the bees are doing what they're supposed to. It's normal."

She wrote back, "Swarms are circling the chimney."

Merde.

This is the *third* time bees have been in that chimney. The first time, firemen—actually a firewoman—climbed a ladder and removed the hive from the chimney. I gave her and the crew a fifty-dollar tip for beer—as they wouldn't accept payment—and they drove off happy and content, my friends for life. The second time a beekeeper removed them and kept the hive. This, the third time, ought to be a charm. "Call Ella," I write, and leave it at that.

Ella is the keeper of the keys and overseer of my house. She's the third English woman—first Louise, then Chris, and now Ella—with a mania for rightness. She is smart, funny, vivacious, pert, competent, creative, practical, pretty, and efficient. She sees a problem, and she fixes it—or gets it fixed, which mostly means telling Rick, her husband, to fix it—and he does. As far as I can see, there's nothing the two of them can't handle. So when I tell Emily to call Ella, I know everything will be all right.

Three days later, Ella emails me. "I can't find a beekeeper. No one will do the job."

"What about the firemen—and women?"

"They won't do it, either."

So much for friends for life. I email Sharon, whose elder son, Yann, is a roofer and apprentice beekeeper. She or he will find someone, I'm sure.

Sharon writes back a week later. "No one will do the work."

I'm amazed. You'd think with all the news about the end-of-the-world honeybee shortages and bees dying from pesticides and being killed by killer bees, someone would want to save them. Apparently not. Why? Because they're in the chimney—which makes no sense to me: they were in my chimney—*this* chimney—twice before, and the firewoman got them the first time, and the beekeeper the second. Why is this time different from the other times? I don't know, but the firemen and women no longer provide the service, and the beekeeper who did it before is gone, and everyone else says it can't be done.

That's when Emily writes, "Honey is dripping down the sides of the chimney."

I call Ella.

Ella calls Rick, who is in their caravan, on vacation with their son Jacob, ninety minutes away, on one of Brittany's many secret beaches. Rick locks everything up and drives back to Plobien. He takes one look at a few dead bees on the floor and the honey dripping down the walls of the chimney and does what most men would do: he covers it up and seals it. He measures the chimney opening, where a damper would be if there was a damper, cuts a piece of wallboard the size of the nonexistent damper, and seals it in place with silicon, then heads back to the caravan and hopefully still secret beach with Ella.

It works, sort of. Bees are still swarming outside the chimney and building their hive inside, but Emily can use the room again, which is how it is when I arrive three weeks later, open the door, see what's happening, and slam it shut. "Holy shit!"

Honey is puddling on my hearth! Honey-Is-Puddling-on-My-Hearth! It sounds better and nicer than it is. I've never seen anything like it, and I hope I never see it again. It's dripping down the walls of the chimney and pooling. From inside the chimney, I hear buzzing. I walk over to listen. It sounds to me like a root canal, something I'm more familiar with than I want to be.

I pick up where Ella and Sharon left off, trying to find a beekeeper who will remove the hive. I turn on my computer—which, thanks to Eric and Manu and Agent Orange, and much to my amazement, continues to work. I type "phone numbers in France," and *Pages Jaunes*—Yellow Pages—pops up. I type "apiculteur"—beekeeper—and my zip code and find twenty-six beekeepers in a fifty-kilometer, thirty-mile, radius. I start calling, and if no one answers, which is most of the time, I leave a message.

"Bonjour. J'ai les abeilles dans le cheminée. C'est possible vous visite chez moi et au revoir les abeilles?" Hello. I have bees in the chimney. It is possible you visit my house and goodbye the bees? I leave my phone number.

I know I could go to Google to translate this and say it correctly—or at least use the correct words in the correct order. I don't because over the years I've learned the better my French, the faster and more detailed people speak, and the more I don't understand, meaning it's better to sound like an idiot and surprise them with what I *do* understand than to sound intelligent and disappoint them with what I don't. This way whomever I speak with or whoever gets the message will have fair warning—like truth in packaging: beware—which is probably why no one returns my call. Nine of the twenty-six have email addresses. I send all of them the same message. None of them writes back, either. The few people who do pick up their phone amazingly allow me to tell my story, and then say, "Désoleé. Ce n'est pas possible."

Even Madame P—Yvonne—knower of all, fixer of everything, can't find anyone. It's like the Dark Ages all over again. Fifteen years ago, it could be done. Now, it can't. I don't know if the bees are more aggressive, or the beekeepers more timid. All I know is I'm two weeks older, I have more honey on my hearth, no hope, and no plan.

I decide to visit the insurance guy. If anything happens to the house, I'll have to go to him anyhow. Besides, insurance people ought to know something about protection.

I see through his window that he's busy, as usual, sitting behind his desk, talking with a client. I open the door and walk in. The woman sitting behind the other desk smiles and rushes around her desk to greet me. I assume she's Annie, his wife. We've exchanged holiday cards for years, but have never met.

"Bonjour," she says, shaking my hand vigorously. "Je suis Annie."

"Bonjour, bonjour," I say. "C'est une grande plaisir." It's a great pleasure, and I ask my usual question, "Vous allez bien?" Are you good?

"Oui, oui . . ." and she points to her husband, Claude.

"Bonjour," I say, wondering if I've been rude, not saying bonjour to him even though he's talking with someone else.

"Bonjour," he says, and stares at me, a very un-French thing to do.

Annie's smiling, he's staring, the woman he's working with is baffled, as neither she nor I have any idea what's going on.

"Regardez," says Annie.

I do. I regard all around me: the office, chairs, desk, computers, out the window, the walls, photos, posters, and don't see anything unusual.

She taps her eyeglasses.

Glasses in France are like jewelry—they *are* jewelry—accoutrements of design and beauty. Hers are ornate and fancy. I guess she wants me to acknowledge them, which is also very rare in France. French people wear gorgeous things to be acknowledged, but they don't *ask* to be acknowledged, which is what Annie seems to be doing.

"Bon," I say. "Belle. J'aime beaucoup," and point to her glasses and smile.

"Non," she says, still smiling, but working harder at it, and points at Claude.

"Ah." *He* has new glasses, which is even odder. She's interrupting his work with a growing less and less happy client to point out his new glasses for me to comment on. "Ah, oui, bon, belle, joli . . ."

"Non, non," she squints and removes her glasses and begins rapidly blinking her eyes. When I still don't respond, she resorts to English, and says, "No more."

Oh! I get it! Claude's wearing glasses. He sees better and doesn't squint or blink anymore. Holy cow! He enjoyed my book *and* all the mentions of his squinting and blinking helped to improve his vision. I feel like a hero, a faith healer, a doctor who performed a miraculous medical feat.

Annie and Claude are looking at me expectantly, waiting for something more. The client-lady is also looking at me, clearly preferring less. I don't know what to do or say, so I blurt, "J'ai les abeilles dans ma cheminée." I have the bees in my chimney.

In unison, all three make that sucking sound that sounds like doom. Annie then suggests the firemen. "Les pompiers, peut-être."

I tell her I already tried.

She calls them anyhow, which under the circumstances, I would do, too. They tell her they don't do bees anymore, and she should call an exterminator.

Bees are becoming an endangered species. Beekeepers are all around me—twenty-six in a thirty-mile radius—and no one can save these bees. "Okay," I shrug, defeated. The environment is one thing, my house and hearth another.

Annie calls two exterminators, explains the situation to each, gives both my name and phone number, and tells them it's urgent, and to call me.

I thank her. "Merci, merci beaucoup," and shake her hand, Claude's hand, and the not-so-happy customer's hand, and leave—and wait.

Either this is exterminator season and these guys have no time for this job, or they've done themselves in. Meanwhile, every day, several times a day, I open the bedroom door, listen to the drilling sound, and watch the honey-pool spread on my hearth. I don't have the heart to go back to Annie, and Ella, Sharon, and Madame P have done what they can, so I keep the bedroom door closed, sleep in the attic, and wait—something I'm slowly, reluctantly, still resistantly, getting better and better at.

Two weeks later, when I've just about reconciled myself to living with the bees, the phone rings.

"Halo, bonjour," I say, and listen to a man speaking very fast. As usual, I don't understand a thing. I'm about to say "Désoleé, je parle français une peu" and hang up, when I hear the word "abeilles." Bees.

Monsieur le Exterminator! "Quand voulez-vous visite chez mois pour les abeilles?" Like I'm inviting him to my house to meet the bee family. He says nothing, which means he already told me everything I need to know, or I just said something weird, or offensive, or all three. "Monsieur?"

"Oui, oui . . . Demain . . . après-midi . . . dix huit heures," he says very slowly. Tomorrow . . . afternoon . . . 6:00 p.m.

I'm elated. I've already got enough honey on my hearth for a double stack of pancakes. "Bien. Bon. Au demain . . . apres midi . . . au dix huit heur," I repeat to assure him I understand, but I think he hung up before I finished.

The next day, a little after 6:00 p.m., a small Renault van pulls into my driveway. A short balding guy in regular street clothes steps out. I'm watching from the second-floor bathroom window. He's looking up at the bees and probably wondering what he's gotten himself into. It's a three-story house—he never asked me about that, or at least I never answered it—and there's no way that van can hold a ladder long enough to reach the roof.

I hurry down the stairs as fast as I can, holding on to the banister, to greet him before he can get away. I open the door, and there he is, standing there, grinning. For an exterminator, he's quite a happy guy. Years before, I had a wasp guy who was dour, which seemed much more appropriate for the job.

"Bonjour," he says, still smiling profusely. I don't know if he's got new dentures, he's been out of work a long time, he *really* enjoys killing things, or he's just friendly. Whatever it is, it's very un-French and unnerving.

"Bonjour," I say and hold out my hand to shake. He shakes my hand and hands me his card, as most French workers do, to prove their bona fides.

"Entrez, entrez," I say, stepping aside while explaining, "Les abeilles habite dans le cheminée. Je cherche pour une aplicuteur, mais tout le personne dit c'est ne pas possible parti le rouche." The bees reside in the chimney. I search for a beekeeper, but everyone say it is not possible to depart the hive. I tell him this so he doesn't think I'm a killer, too.

All the while I'm talking, he's saying, "Si, si, si," like he's heard it all before, though I'm pretty sure not in this particular way. To stop me, he says, "Les abeilles?"

I lead him up the stairs to the second-floor bedroom, open the door, and point to the fireplace and honey-hearth. He says, "Non."

No! After all this, and he's not going to do it? Holy cow.

"La cheminée."

Jesus, is he blind. Maybe *that's* why he's smiling. I point to the chimney. *He* looks at *me* as if *I'm* nuts. He starts to explain, then turns away and walks up the stairs to the attic.

"Monsieur, Monsieur," I call from behind him, "pas le cheminée ce la," and point to the attic. There is no fireplace up there.

He walks to the skylight, opens it, and looks out. I go to the other skylight, open it, and look out. We're both looking at bees swarming the chimney, which we could have seen from the front lawn.

"Bon," he says.

"Bon," I say, except he knows what he is saying and why—at least I hope he does—and I don't.

"Un moment," he says, and goes back down the stairs to his van. The wasp guy did the same thing. He came upstairs to the attic, saw the nest, and returned to his van where he proceeded to cover himself head-to-toes and all of his fingers in protective gear that looked like those old-fashioned deep-sea diving suits complete with helmet and see-through mask. Like this, a modern-day Neptune, he clomped up the stairs, killed the wasps and their progeny, and stayed another ninety minutes bemoaning his fate.

The bee guy returns dressed as he was: a regular guy with no mask, smock, or gloves. He's carrying two poles and a tin cup. It looks to me like safe begging. I didn't watch the wasp guy because his outfit and the wasps scared me. But this guy looks like he's going to the circus, like he's going to balance the cup on the poles on his nose.

I watch him screw the cup onto the end of one pole and the other pole into the first. It looks like he's going to feed sharks. He opens the skylight, sticks the pole out, and adjusts the length, making sure it reaches the chimney. He slides the pole back into the attic, fills the cup with a white powder—like a laundry detergent or Zyklon B—pushes the pole out the window, dumps the powder into the chimney, and says, "C'est tout."

"C'est vrais?" It really is like Zyklon B.

"Oui. Regardez les abeilles."

I look out the window and see the bees flying around, slightly confused, dusted in a powdery sugar, looking sweet, edible, calm.

"Elles seront toutes mortes dans vingt-quatre heures." They'll all be dead in twenty-four hours.

"C'est vrais?"

He looks at me like he's trying to figure out if I'm deaf or dumb or both. I decide not to let him wait for an answer. "Combien?" I ask. How much.

"Cent euros."

The same as the wasp guy. I write him a check and he leaves, but not before I ask him again, "Tout est mort en vingt-quatre heures?"

"Toutes."

And that's that—except I still have the hive, a gazillion dead bees, and honey dripping down the walls in my chimney. Now, instead of being done with this job, as I thought I'd be, I have another problem—and I need to call Monsieur C.

One of the things I admire about a sometimes still-trying-to-be-demi-semi-socialist state is that it provides employment. Take for example, *auto-écoles*, driving schools. They're everywhere, a half dozen in Loscoat alone. Who knows why or what they teach, given how French people drive? I finally ask my friend Gilles, and he tells me, "It's to employ the veterans," which makes sense. In the U.S., we thank them, give them a ribbon or two, then warehouse them, ignore them, leave them on the streets, unhealthy, untreated, untreatable, and unemployed. In France, they hire them. In France, the government *makes* jobs for people, which is why there are all those *auto-écoles*, and why every summer dozens of high school kids are hired to tend the public gardens, water the plants, and weed, and why every year I need to buy an official signed and sealed certificate verifying my chimneys are safe and clean. No certificate, no insurance if my house burns down from a chimney fire, which is the most common kind of fire there is. It's ingenious—and expensive, as there are five chimneys in my house. It's one of the reasons I know Monsieur C. Another is my furnace. Monsieur C is my saint of hot water and heat.

I call him the next day. "Bonjour, Monsieur C."

"Hello, Marc." That and "No problem" are the extent of his English.

"J'ai les abeilles dans la cheminée," I blurt.

"Appelles les pompiers." Call the firemen.

"No, no, tout est mort." They're dead. "Maintenant, c'est necessaire nettoye, mais j'ai une ruche dans le cheminée." Now, it is necessary clean, but I have a hive in the chimney. "C'est possible?"

"Oui."

"Aussi beaucoup de miel." Also lots of honey.

"Oh, la, la . . ." This is the second time I've heard this said. The first time was when I went to the pharmacy because I had diarrhea. The pretty lady asked me how many times a day, and I told her six or eight, and she said, "Oh, la, la." I hope it's not as bad as that.

Three hours later, Monsieur C and his newest assistant park in the driveway. I watch from the second-floor bathroom window—my lookout spot—and see Monsieur C walk to the shed—as he always does when he comes to my house—to check on the furnace he's kept alive all these years. The assistant unloads the van. He pushes a huge, oil barrel-size, industrial vacuum cleaner that looks like a pressure cooker, complete with dials, hoses, nozzles, and brushes, to the front door.

I point him up the stairs to the second-floor bedroom and follow, glad I don't understand what he's muttering. I don't know if Monsieur C has told him what to expect, so I explain.

"Beaucoup les mort abeilles ce la." I tap on the chimney cover Rick sealed in place over a month ago, a cover I have not had the heart or nerve or stomach to go near, let alone touch until now. "*Beaucoup!*"

I see the apprentice looking at the honey on the hearth, probably wondering if I'm a sloppy eater, or if it's really what he thinks it is. "Miel," I confirm. Honey. "Le ruche ce la." I tap on the cover again. The hive here.

He looks at me like (1) are you nuts, and (2) no way. "Un moment," he says, and goes down the stairs and out to the shed to see Monsieur C. Five minutes later, they both march up the stairs. Monsieur C shakes his head and looks at me sadly, seriously, darkly.

"Tout est mort," I say, hopefully. All is dead.

Monsieur C walks over to the chimney and listens. Nothing. He taps, then bangs on Rick's cover. Nothing. He puts his finger in the honey, pushing a few dead bees aside, and tastes it. Then he sends his apprentice downstairs for something. He returns with a long, thin screwdriver, which I know will not work. Rick is a master sealer. When he seals something, it is sealed. This is going to require a box cutter. Sure enough, Monsieur C sends the apprentice back to the van for a knife. I watch, standing near the door, ready to escape, as he cuts the silicon seal, slowly lowers the cover, and thousands of dead bees and bits of hive—honeycomb—like pieces of brain—tumble down onto the hearth. My chimney has become a cemetery. It looks like a death camp, which I guess to the bees it is.

Monsieur C goes back to the furnace, where clearly he would rather be. The apprentice turns on the vacuum, and I watch as he sucks up everything that has fallen—and then begins the real work, cleaning inside the chimney, including the hive that's still there and the honey that's stuck to the walls and still dripping. He uses every brush he has and spends over ninety minutes doing it.

When he's finished and Monsieur C has saved my furnace one more time, we do what we always do: sit at the table, drink coffee, and chat. Actually, Monsieur C chats, I say "Oui" or "Bon" or "Bien sûr" and the apprentice listens. Every few minutes we all laugh, with two of the three of us knowing what we're laughing about. Then, before leaving, as he always does, Monsieur C explains the work he did, why he did it, and how long it will last. In the case of the furnace, he's not guaranteeing anything. It's old, inefficient, and needs to be replaced—three things I don't want to hear. I just want him to keep applying his magic and getting me one more year, a year at a time, as he's done for the past five years.

"Et le cheminée?" I ask. "Nettoye?" Clean?

"Oui."

"Pas d'abeilles et le ruche." No bees and hive?

"Parti." Gone.

"Et le miel dans l'interior?" And the honey in the inside?

He gives me that palm-down wavy hand motion that means so-so, maybe, probably not. Then he explains: "Grosse ruche . . ." Big hive . . . "Beaucoup d'abeilles habitent dans la cheminée depuis longtemps . . ." Many bees live in the chimney long time. "Beaucoup de miel . . ." Lots of honey . . . and he shows me how it sticks, is glued in the crannies and grooves of the chimney's stone walls. "Impossible de tout nettoyer . . ." It's not possible to clean it all.

"C'est bon pour le feu?" It's good for the fire, I ask. Meaning, is it safe to have a fire, not will the fire like it?

"No problème," and he hands me the bill and a signed and sealed certificate, verifying the chimney is safe for another year, and if there's a fire, my insurance will cover it.

Then, as he's leaving, I ask him the one question that matters most, the question I've been thinking about since Emily first wrote to me, the question I've been afraid to ask, because I already know the answer, "Les abeilles revenir?" The bees come back?

He gives me that palm-down wavy handshake, which this time means (1) of course they will (there's honey on the walls, they've been in that chimney three times, they'll definitely be back next spring), and (2) I don't have the heart to tell you.

There's only one thing left to do. I call Madame P, and after telling her the weather is good, "C'est bon, la meteo," (which she can see for herself out her window), I add: "C'est neces-saire je ferme le cheminée." It is necessary I close the chimney. "Connais-vous un personne fait le travail?" Know you a person make the work?

"Oui. Bien sûr," and she gives me the name and phone number of a local fellow, using the magic words "un artisan" and "bon travail."

It took four weeks to get rid of the bees and have the chimney cleaned. In the U.S., I'd be frustrated, angry, and stressed. In France, I'm optimistic. I'm close to the end, I think. I can see the finish line, I think—and I want the house fixed and pretty, ready for Donna when she arrives. . . I call the number and leave a message.

"Bonjour, Monsieur. J'ai les abeilles dans ma cheminée trois fois. C'est necessaire ferme le cheminée en haut, dans le exte-rior, avec cement." I have bees in my chimney three times. It is necessary close the chimney on high, in the outside, with cement." Pretty clear, I think.

Maybe not. There's no response. I wait a few days and call again, leaving the same message, adding, "Madame P donne moi votre nom," Madame P give me your name, hoping to shame or guilt or fear him to respond.

No way.

I wait another another few days, call again, and begin call-ing other numbers I find in the yellow pages for *zinguers*—metalworkers—the guys who do this kind of work. No one answers the phone, and no one returns my messages.

Three days later, I'm sitting on the terrace, drinking my afternoon coffee, reading and trying to understand Stephen Hawking's *On Time*, when three guys who look like they're straight out of the Sinaloa cartel and they're here for a hostage taking, ransom, or worse, saunter onto my yard. They have closely cropped skinhead hair, tattoos on their arms, hands, fingers, neck—who knows where else?—and multiple piercings. In the U.S., I'd run inside and hide. In Brittany, I say, "Bonjour," though with a bit of trepidation.

"Bonjour. Monsieur Greenseed? Nous sommes ici pour la cheminée," and the leader of the pack hands me his card. I take it and read the name, amazed. *THESE* are the guys Madame P recommended? I know she has a great tolerance for deviance—I'm proof of that—but this! *This* isn't Frommer's or my mother's or my France. Only, I guess, it is.

I turn my back to them and lead them up the stairs—two other things I'd never do in the U.S. I open the bedroom door and show them the chimney. "Beaucoup les abeilles. Trois fois. C'est necessaire ferme le cheminée en haut en l'exterior," and I point up to let them know I want the chimney sealed from the top, not inside the house, but *outside*. "En haut, l'exterior," I emphasize.

One after the other, they take turns looking up the chimney. What the hell? I look up, too. It's black. We go back downstairs, and I turn right, into the kitchen to discuss price, as I always do when discussing house work with potential workers. They turn left, into the TV/sitting room, which is very suspicious and odd: French people don't usually go anywhere—enter a house, room, terrace, take a plate, glass of wine, or hors d'oeuvres—without being invited, encouraged, sometimes begged to do so, and these guys just marched into the room.

The guy who handed me the business card, the leader, I assume, moves the fireplace screen and looks up the chimney. Then, one at a time, probably in some hierarchical order, all of the others look up, too. It's like the Keystone Cops meet

Sinaloa: there's lots of discussion and hand wriggling; the only thing missing is Larry, Curly, and Moe and a couple of head bops. Finally, the leader—having long ago determined that language is useless—asks, "Avez-vous du papier et un stylo?"

I give him a piece of paper and a pen, thinking, it's a chimney, for God's sake. Just climb the ladder and seal the damned thing.

He draws six vertical lines, the outer lines shorter, thicker and bolder than the inner, something that looks like an unfinished house.

Then he shades three areas, adds a thin horizontal line, bisecting the vertical lines through the middle, and writes the numbers 1 and 2.

I have no idea until he adds two curlicues.

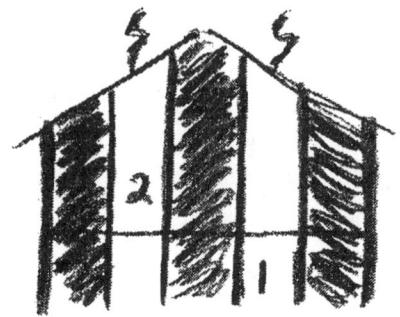

Smoke. I get it. Smoke is coming from the first-floor fireplace in the TV/sitting room, # 1, and from the second-floor fireplace in the bedroom with the bees, # 2. What I don't get is why all the detail and explanation. Either this guy is extraordinarily thorough and conscientious, or he thinks I'm a moron—or both. This is what I'm thinking when he draws an arrow from fireplace #1 to the left and another from fireplace # 2 to the right—

—and I immediately understand all that looking up into the dark chimneys.

Normally—my normal, not French normal—the fireplace flue is directly above the fireplace. But not here. Here the drafts cross. Fireplace #1, on the first floor, vents left, and fireplace #2, on the second floor, vents right, meaning the opening to be sealed on top is the one closest to the front of the house, not the one in the rear, *not* the one directly over the second-floor bedroom, the one I would have sealed. I'm dumbfounded, and these guys are geniuses.

He tells me the price, and for the first time ever I say, "Je suis un ecrivan," I'm a writer, and I tell them about *Jamais Je Ne Serai Français*, the French translation of *I'll Never Be French* because I *do* want them to think what I'll write about them, though it doesn't seem to register or matter. They promise to return in three days—a day before Donna arrives—and, amazingly, they do. They are pleasant, professional, quick, clean, efficient, and gone.

It took six weeks, but it's done. I'm elated. I celebrate with a DVD of *Slaughterhouse-Five*, an anchovy pizza, expensive Haut-Médoc, and a fire in the fireplace. In five minutes, the room is full of smoke. They sealed the wrong fireplace! They-sealed-the-wrong-chimney!

The next morning, I call the guy back. "Bonjour. C'est Monsieur Greenseed. C'est un problem. Vous-avez ferme les cheminée dans le rez-de-chaussée, pas le premier étage." It is a problem. You have close the chimney in the ground floor, not the first floor (which is the second floor in the U.S.).

They return in the afternoon, break the cement seal, return my money, and leave without suggesting or offering to seal the correct chimney, which means I'm back where I started and the bees will return in the spring. I'm envisioning a lifetime relationship with the smiling exterminator.

A few days later, while Donna is sleeping off the nine-hour time difference, ten-hour flight, and twenty-three hours of door-to-door travel, Monsieur Charles knocks on the door. All along, I've been telling him what's been happening. Now, I tell him the latest. When I'm done—after showing him the drawings and making waving motions with my hands to indicate the crisscrossing flues, he says, "J'ai un ami." I have a friend . . . .

Monsieur M arrives the next day with a ladder, a bag of cement, and hoods for the chimneys—called *chapeaus*—hats, to keep embers from escaping. He seals the correct chimney, covers that chimney and three others with *chapeaus*, and it's done.

No more bees and one less chimney for Monsieur C to clean. A win-win if there ever was one, except maybe for the bees. Monsieur M shows me the seal is thick enough to keep the bees out, and—making a tapping motion with a ball-peen hammer—thin enough to be easily broken, allowing me a bee-free future or a reopened chimney, whichever I prefer. "Comme vous-voulez," he says. As I want, as if the choice was mine and not the bees'.

Now, every time I enter the house and every time I leave, I look up. The bees haven't returned yet, but I suspect they will, either to that chimney or one of the others, and then I'll have to do this all over again.

In the U.S., we like to think we're free of history, that every day is, or can be, or *should* be the first day of the rest of your life. Not so in France. In France, the past isn't over or forgotten so much as moved on—a building-on rather than erasing: on and on and on until in a year or a decade or a century, it returns—as I expect the bees will, and when they do, I'll call the *pompiers*, because in a year, or three, or fifty, they'll probably be doing this work again. This is what I expect. What I don't expect is a problem paying my electric bill—and I'm beginning to wonder if there are some challenges and growth opportunities not worth having and/or best to avoid . . . .

EDF, Electricité de France

Madame P—Yvonne—knocks on my door, says "Bonjour," and hands me an envelope with a red border. It's not my birthday or a holiday, so I know it can't be good.

"Bonjour," I say, give her four cheek kisses, and invite her in, "Entrez, entrez." She declines, saying she has a doctor's appointment. More and more our conversations are about doctors and health. Health talk has replaced weather and politics and daily news. Health talk *is* the daily news.

I walk her back to her car, holding her arm, each of us walking slowly: she because her foot is swollen and achy; me because my lower back hurts from sitting at the computer too long, tying my shoelaces, lifting groceries, or something worse. I open her car door, give her four more cheek kisses, say, "à tout à l'heure," and wave as she peels out and races off to see her doctor. Then I go back to the house to see what's in the letter I haven't stopped thinking about since she gave it to me.

I rip the envelope open and read *Dernier Notice*, final notice, in large bold script. Holy Christ! It says I owe EDF 306 euros. I look at the date: March 20. It's now June 12. The bill is for the *previous* six-month billing period, June to January, which means I haven't paid anything for thirteen months. In the U.S., I'd already be in the dark. Who knows how much longer I have in France? I call Sharon and tell her, "I just got a *dernier notice* bill from EDF for 306 euros that's three months overdue."

"Don't worry," she says, knowing that I will, I do, I am, "they're not going to cut off your electricity."

I'm too American to believe her. After all, they sent a letter that says *final* notice in big letters dated more than three months ago for electricity received more than a year ago. I need to pay this bill today, then remember it's Monday and most business offices are closed on Mondays.

Early the next morning I drive to the local EDF office in Loscoat, a place I've been numerous times. It's locked and no one is there. I know public agencies have strange hours and aren't always open when they say they will be, so I'm not surprised, though this is the first time this has happened with EDF.

I make numerous trips to the office, mornings, afternoons, early evenings, Saturday, and each time it is locked and no one is there. There are prominent signs on the gate and door saying EDF, which I think means they haven't moved, but I can't be sure, because there's still a prominent sign for a boulangerie in Plobien that burned down twenty-five years ago and never reopened and was never replaced. I don't know what else to do, so like the crazy person who keeps doing the same thing hoping for a different outcome, I keep driving to the office hoping to pay the bill and forestall the darkness I know is coming.

On my umpteenth try, I see a fellow loading equipment onto an EDF truck. Eureka, I think, and voilà! I walk toward the office with my checkbook and *Dernier Notice* in hand, ready to put an end to this story.

"C'est fermé," the fellow calls. Closed.

"Quand ouvert?" When open?

"Jamais. C'est fermé." Never.

"Okay. Merci."

I figure they must have consolidated—too many small, local offices—the way Orange/France Telecom used to have an office in Loscoat, but now I have to go to Quimper to find them. I drive to Pont-de Buis, Le Faou, Plougastel-Daoulas, and all of the EDF offices are fermés.

"What's up?" I ask Sharon. "I've been to all the local EDF offices and they're all closed."

"They've gone the American way."

I know from the way she says it that it's not a good way to go. "What's that?" I ask.

"They shut all the offices to save money."

"Even the regional offices in Quimper, Brest, Nantes, and Morlaix?"

"*All.* You have to contact them by mail, phone, or internet."

Merde.

All my other regular bills—garbage, phone, internet, water—are automatically deducted from my checking account. I haven't yet automated this one because it only comes twice a year, and I pay it by check. Two checks, one every six months. It's worked fine for years, but this time—who knows why?—the bill, which has always been sent to the U.S., didn't arrive, and since it only comes twice a year, I didn't remember it, miss it, or pay it. The *Dernière Notice* was sent to Plobien, and it either languished in the empty house until Madame P found it, or it was forwarded to her house, and it languished there because she forgot to forward it to me. Either way, the bill is seriously, dangerously overdue.

I reread the letter and see lots of words but no address telling me where to send my check. I open the yellow pages of the phone book and find every listing except EDF. I open the white pages and flip through eleven pages of public service listings—birth certificates, death certificates, passports, identity cards, divorce, auto registration, transportation schedules, international codes for phone calls, emergency numbers for police, fire, ambulances—and find nothing for EDF.

I go online, type *EDF*, and search the website thinking I'll enter my name and address, access my account, and pay the bill. Ha! No way. I need my account number to access my account, but I don't have my account number because it's on the bill they didn't send with the *Dernier Notice*, and since I normally pay the bill in the U.S. all of the past bills are there, not here.

I call Donna, knowing she's asleep, hoping I wake her or she listens to her messages before she goes to work. "Hi, Sweetie, can you look through last year's tax receipts and find an EDF bill and send me the account number?" I say this as if it's easy, normal, like opening a drawer and finding a spoon, but I know it's not. I also know I may not get the information for at least a day and maybe two, and I'm certain my time is running out. I have visions of the lights going off, water turning cold, losing the best sentence, paragraph, page I ever wrote—food spoiling in the fridge, mold growing on the undehumidified walls . . .

I go back to searching for information online, for anything that could help, and to my amazement I see a link that says *EDF in English*. Holy cow! I click on it and sure enough there's the EDF cover page in English. I go to the drop-down menu and then to *My Account*, hoping it will tell me how to pay the bill, and it drops me into French and doesn't tell me anything I need to know. It explains how to read the bill that I don't have and says nothing about how to pay the bill, which you'd think they'd care most about, but apparently don't. All I can figure is France joined the internet economy five years too soon, I need more brain cells, or both. It's like bobbing for apples in the ocean.

I keep searching the *EDF in English*, really in French, cover page and its attachments, and, miracle of miracles, see *Telephone Number for EDF in English.* With not much hope or enthusiasm, I call it, and in no time at all a voice with a British accent says, "Welcome to EDF international. For English . . ." and it breaks into French. I wait a moment and hear the all-too-familiar "Please stay on the line, your call will be answered shortly," for the next thirty minutes and hang up.

There's nothing left to do but call Sharon. "Can you find the number and call EDF and ask them what I'm supposed to do to pay the bill?"

She calls back an hour later. "I've been on hold for an hour. I can't wait any longer. I'll try again next week."

Next week! By then I'll be showering in cold water and eating soggy, spoiled food in the dark. Thankfully, three of the burners on my stove are gas. "Okay," I say. "What's their number?"

She gives it to me and I call, and once again I enter French automatic dialing. "For X tapez un. For Y tapez deux." In the U.S., when I enter this world I start yelling into the phone. In France, I call the number again and again, at least twenty-five times, making numerous errors, trying to get the right sequence, until, luckily, I get an operator who knows enough English to tell me the numbers I need to push. No, she can't help me with my problem—how to pay the damn bill—but she can get me to the right office.

"Merci," I say, hang up, call the same number again, tapez my way through the sequence she gave me, and hear the French version of "Your call is very important to us, please stay on the line . . ." Given what French people do with lines, I'm pretty sure it doesn't say, "Your call will be answered in the order in which it was received," and even if it did, I wouldn't believe it. I listen to this for the next thirty, forty, forty-five minutes, until someone answers the phone, "Bonjour."

"Bonjour, madame. J'ai une problem."

"Oui."

"EDF envoi moi une lettre demande je payee une facture." EDF send me a letter asking I pay a bill.

"Votre numéro de compte." Your account number.

"Je ne sais pas." I don't know.

She sighs. "Votre nom." Your name.

I sigh. I never pronounce the letters correctly. I'm thinking Greenside, pronounced JRIINSEDI, when I blurt, "Parlez-vous anglais?"

"Yes, a little."

Holy cow. Pay dirt! I explain about the letter, the amount I owe, that I never received the bill, how I tried to pay it at a local EDF office, but they're all closed, and I tried online, and now, thankfully I found her.

"Oui," she says.

"Can I pay by TIP," the automatic deduction system I use to pay my other bills.

"Yes, but not this bill." She explains I can pay future bills by TIP. This bill, being past due and not prior TIP authorized, must be paid by check. She then gives me my account number and the address of the customer services office in Lyon where I need to send the check along with my RIB (whatever the hell that stands for) to authorize all future automatic payments by TIP (whatever the hell that means).

I'm thrilled. Overjoyed. Amazed. I thank her profusely. Then I write a letter in English explaining everything I said to the lady and Google-translate it into French, so who knows what it actually says. I write a check for 306 euros, not knowing or caring if it includes penalties, late fees, and interest. I include their dernier letter and my RIB (that I find in my checkbook) to authorize the TIP, the automatic deduction of future bills. I print the address she gave me in Lyon and my return address on a manila envelope, make a copy of everything, and mail it registered mail, receipt requested, as I'm not taking any chances, though I've never had a problem with the mail in France before.

I mail it on June 23. On June 26, I receive a signed and stamped confirmation of receipt from Monsieur Henri.

Voilà!

I return to my regular life which, unfortunately for my bank, includes weekly visits to get money. I know I can get money from an ATM but I don't want to, because try as I have to raise my limit—and I have, repeatedly—I can still only withdraw 400 euros per week from my account, and I don't want to reduce that reserve in case there's an actual emergency and I need them. So once a week I go to my local branch and withdraw money directly, in person, which seems to not have a weekly limit—and because my bank statement is sent to me in the U.S. (where I am nine months of the year), and I never know how much is in the account (because of all the automatic deductions), I'm constantly worried about being overdrawn, which is why every weekly exchange ends like this:

"S'il vous plaît, donnez moi un copie a ma compte?" Please, give me a copy at my account. This is how, three weeks later, I discover the check to EDF has not been cashed.

I figure it's a large corporation and my check must be making its way through the chain. After all, even in the U.S., Doctors Without Borders and Partners in Health often take that much time or longer to cash my checks, though Planned Parenthood manages to do it in days.

Three weeks later, six weeks after I mailed the check, it's still not cashed.

Now, I'm worried. The *Dernière Notice* is five months old, the original bill, which goes back fifteen months, is eight months overdue, Donna is coming, and she probably expects the house to have electricity.

I look for the telephone number I saved because seventy years have taught me whenever I throw something away I'll need it in a day, week, month, or decade. I open my EDF folder, find the number, and call—and when someone answers on the third ring, I hope and beg, "Parlez vous anglais?"

"Yes," a woman answers.

I explain everything that happened, telling her, "I always pay my bills on time, and I tried to pay this one, but all the offices are closed, and six weeks ago I mailed a check for 306 euros with my RIB for the TIP and future automatic payments, but when I look at my bank account I see the check hasn't been cashed and I'm worried because I'm going to the U.S. soon, and I want to pay this bill before I leave."

"Your account number?

I look through my papers and tell her the number.

"Mr. Greenside?"

"Yes."

"Your bill hasn't been paid."

"Oui," I say, hoping French—even *my* French—will soften her. "That's why I'm calling you. I mailed the bill and a check on June 23. I have the signed and stamped confirmation from Customer Service in Lyon to prove it."

"From where?"

"Customer Service in Lyon."

"That's not correct."

"It's not EDF?"

"Yes, but it's not where you pay your bills."

I don't say "EDF gave me that address," or "Couldn't someone forward it to the right office?"

She doesn't say anything, either.

"Okay. *Where* should I send it?"

She gives me an address in Paris.

"How much is the bill now?" figuring more late fees, interest, and penalties.

"306 euros."

"Merci," I say, and write the check and another cover letter, once again explaining everything that happened and why. Then I ask Sharon to also write a message so they don't think my illiterate Google note is a ransom note or a hoax. I address the envelope to the Paris address and mail it certified, receipt requested. Three days later I receive the signed and stamped confirmation of its receipt by Monsieur Yves. The next day I go to the bank to cancel the check that went to Lyon and request, "une copie ma compte, s'il vous plaît." On the bottom of the page, the last item posted is the check for 306 euros. I hope it was cashed by EDF and not Monsieur Yves.

Since then, everything has worked well. I auto-pay my bill by TIP and have an online EDF account I never look at. I receive regular notices from EDF, which I regularly ignore—until today. Today, for some inexplicable reason, I open the notice and try to read it, and when I can't, I do something even more inexplicable—knowing better, knowing I shouldn't, knowing about the cat and curiosity—I decide to see what, if anything, has changed on EDF's website, and if the changes are for better or worse.

I type *EDF* into Google search, and there it is. I click on the link, and it opens—in English! I'm amazed. I read down the page and find links for *Business, My Account, How to Pay Your Bill*—online, by debit, credit, check, paypoint, payzone, post office, even American Express. There's a chat box if I need help and a link to *Difficulty Paying Your Bill, Understanding Your Bill*, and *Direct Debit*, which must be new language for auto deduction, TIP, and RIB. There's even a telephone number for a live chat, and *everything* is in English.

I click on *How to Pay Your Bill* and *By Check By Post* and read, "Make the check payable to EDF, Energy Customers LTD, and send to P.O. Box 140, Plymouth." Plymouth! No wonder this is all in English. This is EDF England. I didn't even know there was an EDF in England. I thought the F stood for France, Electricité de France.

As usual for me in France, I'm back at the start of the circle. Normally, at this point I'd quit, especially since this is a theoretical exploration, not a necessitated one like searching for a beekeeper—but I'm retired now and have lots of time and need to birth or rebirth millions of new brain cells if I'm going to be the French Methuselah.

I type *EDF France* into Google search, and there it is, *EDF (Electricité de France) English Speaking Customer.* I open the page and everything *is* in English: good English, clear English, helpful English, organized English. It's clearer than the web page of Pacific Gas and Electric in California and Con Edison in New York. (I know because I looked.) It's amazing—a trillion prayers come true: there's an English-speaking customer service *Helpline* with a list of the best hours and days to call (Fridays, Saturdays, and in the evenings from six to nine). There's also a list of ways to reach EDF: by phone, online, post, and regional delegation, which seems to mean the regional offices they closed are now open. Most amazingly, it provides an address for complaints— as if they really want to hear them—and another for mediation services. I look through the site and see a link to *Why Call EDF.*

I click on it and then on *Ask Questions About Your Bill.* Four pages of information appear, including *Structure of the Bill, Understanding the Bill,* and a *French-English Glossary* of terms, like *abonnement* (subscription, monthly charge; *relevé* (meter reading); *facture* (bill). Everything is here except *How to Pay Your Bill.*

At the end, there's a box for making comments and/or asking questions. I write: How do I pay an overdue bill? Then I scroll down the page and read other people's comments:

I have written to edf several times about my bill but do not seem to get anywhere with them. DL

For the past 2 days I have been logging on to the french EDF site, trying to pay my bill. I have tried everything but nothing works. It should be so simple! I press the 'payer mon facture' button and nothing happens!!! GR

I am having exactly the same problem! It worked last year using my IBAN number from Moneycorp. I've tried emailing them in French three times and they just say they tried to contact me and to call them instead.

The EDF english speaking numbers don't work on this page too. GP

Same problem for me. I've also had a problem recently when the bill arrives the date to pay it by has either passed or is the next day. I Tried to explain this in an email but not getting very far. CR

I had the same problem. I tried the number above and it doesn't work . . . NM

I am trying yet again to give EDF france my meter readings and access to website is not available anyone else having problems? JL

Since may 2017 i am not able anymore to login to EDF. I still got postal and electronic mailings to pay my bills. I have mailed 4 times to serviceclient@edf.fr but they don't even answer. Their French phone support says they can't even find my client number (anymore). But it must be a technical issue because now I received another letter for late payment. . . It's driving me crazy:) FD

Two weeks later, my question—How to pay an overdue bill?— has not been answered.

This is how it is as I get older: more questions and fewer answers. . . . I'm sorry and surprised to find my big picture is shrinking: I'm focusing less on the earth and the White House, and more on family, friends, muscles, and ligaments. I'm still able to climb to the top of a lighthouse and church steeple, walk six miles a day, and drive three hours at night—though preferably not on the same day.

I've been thinking about Methuselah again. For some reason, I've always assumed he was smart, that those 969 years led to wisdom and understanding, but when I search the Bible—Genesis 5:21–27—there's no mention of intelligence or wisdom, nothing other than age, so now I'm thinking what if he wasn't smart or wise or kind or generous, what if he was just old, an old senile drooler in wet diapers that haven't been changed in seven hundred years—and lately I've been wondering about what's coming next and when? That's the cosmic question. The earthly answer, I hope, minimally, is Monsieur C and soon.

III

Save something from the time where we will never be again.
—Annie Ernaux, *The Years*

Monsieur C

The last person at the house last year—Kathleen—emailed me about the sudden lack of hot water. I told her to push the button on the furnace and hold it, and if the burner didn't ignite— or explode, I didn't say—call Monsieur C, my ever-ready, trustworthy, totally reliable plumber-friend.

I met him years before when I had a problem with my *bac dégraisseur*, though at the time I didn't know I had a *bac dégraisseur*, or what it does. For twenty years, I stepped on it and walked around it—a three-foot long, two-foot wide, three-inch thick cement slab placed in the middle of the concrete path that encircles the house, never once wondering what was inside. It's like those water and sewer cement covers in front of houses in the U.S.—*something* is under there, but whatever it is, it's someone else's business, not mine—and that's how I thought of my French cement cover until the day before Donna and I were returning to California, and I went to bring the terrace furniture in for storage, and smelled demise.

Plobien is a small town within a regional park. It's rural, and there are lots of farms and animals nearby. I've smelled many things over the years, the worst being pigs knowing they're on their way to market and the industrial chickens in a factory a mile away—and this stench was worse than those. This stench was something else: forget Hemingway, *this* was death in the afternoon.

I walked around the yard looking for something dead—something large and dead and decomposing—or, maybe, on the bright side (I hoped), Monsieur Charles finally wiped out the mole metropolis living under, deconstructing, and re-landscaping what used to be my beautiful lawn. I'm walking around looking through bushes, into tunnels and holes, flattening craters and mounds, and see nothing. I walk back toward the house. The closer I get, the stronger the smell. I follow my nose and see the source: a puddle of reeking water seeping from under the cement slab, slowly, incrementally increasing in size and smell. The good news is I don't think it's sewage; the bad news is I don't know what it is, and it smells worse.

I run into the house and call Madame P. "Bonjour, Yvonne. J'ai une problem a la maison. Dans l'exterior j'ai un peu l'eau avec pas bonne perfume." I have a problem at home. In the exterior I have a little water with not good perfume.

"Téléphone Monsieur C."

"Qui?"

"Monsieur C, le plombier, il est un artisan," and using single digits and speaking slowly she gives me his phone number: neuf, huit, huit, six, zero . . .

I call and leave a message. "Bonjour, Monsieur C. Je suis Monsieur Greenseed, l'americain habite en Plobien . . . " I'm the only American in the village, and after *I'll Never Be French* was published in French, and I received a letter addressed to me in Plobien (a fictional village) at Kostez Gwer (a nonexistent address), I'm fairly certain most people know who and where I am . . . "J'ai un problem avec l'eau dans le exterior et je parti France demain." I have a problem with the water in the outside and I leave France tomorrow. In the U.S., I would never tell a worker I've never met that I'm leaving the country the next day, but in Plobien it doesn't matter. The car is gone, my shutters are closed, the gate is locked, and everyone knows everything anyhow.

An hour later there's a knock on the door. I open it. Standing in front of me is a short, stocky, dark-haired fellow wearing regular clothes, not blue worker overalls, who—like me—hasn't shaved in days. He's built like a halfback and looks serious, and except for the facial growth—and his handshake, which is a vise—he could be selling insurance. Actually, he *is* insurance, but I don't know that then.

"Monsieur C?" I ask, just to be sure.

"Oui. Monsieur Greenseed?"

"Oui," I say, and lead him to the side of the house, embarrassed by the smell and the leak, as if they were mine—me— *my* fault and personal failing, which it turns out they are.

"Bon," he says when he sees the puddle, not in the least surprised. I don't know if he's nonchalant because I'm American, and this is what foreigners are expected to do, or because it's no big deal, nothing new, and he sees it every day. I'm hoping for the latter, but expect the former.

He pushes the cement cover off the lip and releases a plume of putrescence: Think rotten eggs and double it. I gag, cover my mouth and nose with my hand, and step back. He kneels and gets closer. I figure he's a plumber, and he's seen and smelled lots worse. Somehow, that comforts me—but not for long. He slides the cover away and exposes a tank of stagnant, scuzzy, rancid, polluted water. He dips a branch in the water and stirs—all I can think is "double, double, toil and trouble" as icebergs of solidified fat and grease, like chunks of frozen whale blubber, rise to the surface and sink.

"Qu'est-ce que c'est?" I ask. What is it?

This is how I learn I have a *bac dégraisseur*—a grease trap—and what *it* does, and *I* didn't.

Rural France (maybe rural everywhere) has this ingenious water filtering system. Unbeknownst to me (as most things seem to be), my kitchen sink drains into a pipe that feeds into a tripart filtering system that through some combination of magic, chemistry, and physics separates the gunk from the water, allowing clean water to flow freely into the septic tank—unless, of course, you never clean the system, as I haven't in twenty-plus years, allowing grease and fat to grow into glaciers that break into icebergs that block the flow of water into the septic tank, causing the *dégraisseur* to overflow, puddle, and stink.

He swirls the stick to show me a chunk of blubber lodged in the bend of the exit pipe, blocking the water and causing the overflow. With a long-handled screwdriver, he picks at the grease and sees it will take him all day. He blasts it with an air compressor and barely Kirk-Douglas-dimples-it. He drills a snake-like thingie into the heart of it and stalls. He then does what I want to do: he bangs the hell out of the pipe to dislodge the fat, and when that doesn't work, he takes a saw from his toolbox and does elbow replacement surgery, cutting out the blocked one and replacing it with a new, clear one that works.

"*Voilà!*" he says, and stands. Then, seeing the look of chagrin and disgust on my face, he kneels and does what I'm sure he would for any disadvantaged person—which clearly he's observed me to be. He scoops out the remaining chunks of fat, puts them in a plastic garbage bag, and leaves me with a good-as-new 150 year old tripart *bac dégraisseur* that I fear and worry about until I get the new sewer connection that bypasses the *dégraisseur.* At least, I think it does. I *hope* it does. I could lift the cover to find out, but I won't.

He packs his tools away and puts them in his van. Then, to my surprise, he gets in the van and starts the engine.

"Monsieur," I wave my checkbook, "La facture!"

"L'année prochaine," he calls as he drives away—and he's right.

The next year he fixes a leak in the attic toilet.

The following year he replaces the toilet on the second/first floor with a new, designer signature toilet—yes, an actual signature on the tank, as French people seem to like haute-couture flourishes even on their plumbing. He also replaces the second-first-floor bathroom sink faucet and stops leaks in the kitchen faucet and shed, where the washing machine lives.

All the while he's nurturing, sustaining, and life-supporting my furnace, which was old when I bought the house.

Kathleen, who emailed me about the lack of hot water, called him three times. Each time, he came and fixed it: cleaning the burner; replacing a part; making adjustments. Once, he even brought her a portable heater from his own house. Every time she called, he came, and every time he came he fixed it, and every time he fixed it, something else went wrong. By the time she left, she was calling him "Charlie," something I haven't had the nerve to do in the ten years I've known him.

Luckily, the weather was warm, and Kathleen was gracious and understanding, and when I refunded several hundred dollars, she was even more so.

Now, I'm here and trying to decide if I need a new furnace. Yesterday, my shower was lukewarm—never a good sign, as usually the hot water is endless—and this morning it was cold. I don't know if I should go for another short-term fix, hoping to get through another year without a new furnace, or pay for a new one now. All I know is I want hot water.

I call Monsieur C, which for me is like calling 911 and AAA at the same time. Amazingly, he knows who it is, and he still answers, "Bonjour, Marc."

"Bonjour, Monsieur C. Encore le problem avec le chauffage. Pas d'eau chaude." Another problem with the heater. No hot water.

Forty minutes later, he arrives and fixes the furnace. Afterward, sitting in the kitchen drinking coffee, he gives me what I'm hoping is a forensics report, not an autopsy. "Le brûleur ne fonctionne pas . . ." The burner doesn't work. "Le chauffage est vieux et peu efficace . . ." The furnace is old, not efficient. "Cela consomme beaucoup de carburant, ce qui est cher, et les réparations sont coûteuses." It uses lots of fuel, which is expensive, and it's expensive to repair.

None of this is new or unexpected, but it's not what I want to hear. "Combien pour tout?" I reluctantly ask. "Le nouveau brûleur, l'installation, et le travail pour le femme l'année derniere." How much for all. A new burner, the installation, and the work for the woman last year?

"Huit cents euros."

A thousand dollars—and I'd still have an old, expensive, inefficient furnace and need a new one in a year or two anyhow. The sewer connection wasn't as expensive as I feared, but a furnace? I see another $5,000 floating away as I swallow, and ask the question I've been hoping to avoid for almost thirty years. "Combien pour le nouveau chauffage?"

"Huit mille euros."

Ten thousand dollars! Holy shit! When Donna replaced her California water heater *and* furnace—two separate devices and systems—it cost a third of that. I point to my head, and say, "Je ponce. Je voudrais téléphoné vous en une semaine." I sand down. I would like to call you in a week. Turns out poncer—ponce—means to sand; the word I want is penser—pense—to think.

All week I pense: spend $1,000 now and continue as I have been for another year or two and hope for the best, which could also become the worst: the one thousand could easily become two or three thousand over the next two years; the price of the new furnace could increase, as could the price and use of fuel, burning more and more, faster and faster in my increasingly older and inefficient furnace—so the choice is really between ten thousand dollars now and thirteen to fifteen thousand in two years, not to mention having no heat and taking freezing showers, neither of which will make Donna or me happy.

A week later I call Monsieur C. "Okay. D'accord—le nouveau chauffage. C'est existe le garantie?"

"Bien sûr," he says. "Dix ans." Ten years. Since the house is usually shut six months a year, I figure that means twenty. I don't ask—as I always do in the U.S.—if the warranty is from the manufacturer, the shop where I purchased the item, or the installer, and if it includes parts and labor and replacement value. I do tell him my dilemma, though.

"J'ai ne pas d'argent." I don't have money. "J'ai trois mille euros maintenant et je voudrais payee le total en autumn." I have three thousand euros now and would like to pay the total in autumn. Basically, I'm asking him for a $7,000 loan that—trust me—I'll pay back at some unspecified date between

September and December, after the work is done and I'm in another country six thousand miles away—and he says exactly what I knew he would.

"Okay. No problème." No papers, either. No contract. No signature. No handshake or eyeball to eyeball. My word on the telephone and his.

"Quand commence le travail?" When start the work?

"Dans une semaine, dix jours." Seven to ten days.

"Combien jours pour le travail?" How many days for the work?

"Trois jours." Three days to put in a furnace! I don't get it. When Donna had the furnace installed, it took half a day, and cleaning and repairing the ducts a couple of hours more.

The next day, the old furnace, feeling betrayed and/ or wanting revenge, gives up the ghost and dies. Kaput. It's unseasonably hot—ninety degrees—and I'm well past ripe to runny. For a week, I go to bed smelly and sweaty and wake up the same. The good news is the washing machine runs on cold water. The bad news is I don't. I change my routine from 6:00 a.m. showers to afternoon after the beach showers, hoping the new furnace arrives before the inevitable rains come and the temperature drops to the fifties.

On the ninth day without hot water, I return from the beach and find $10,000 worth of parts spread on the lawn like a jigsaw puzzle. No wonder it takes three days to install. I'm surprised it doesn't take a month. Monsieur C isn't installing the furnace, he's building it. He's building the new one *and* dismantling the old.

Three days later, exactly as he said, I'm standing in front of my new four-foot-high, three-foot-wide, strawberry-red furnace that looks like a cross between a vertical fire engine and a top-of-the-line espresso machine: lights are blinking, pipes extruding, knobs, switches, valves, and gauges. . . . He walks me through: the pipes—red and blue—and their cut-off valves to regulate the hot water and radiators; the pressure gauge (0–10) and where to set it in summer—1—and winter—3—and never, ever, above 5, or boom; the water temperature gauge set at 55, which I think is ridiculously low and needlessly frugal until he reminds me it's Centigrade and 131 degrees Fahrenheit; four blinking green lights, one of which tells me the furnace is on, the other three I haven't a clue, but as long as they're green, it's okay. The most important information he saves for last: the function knob. The dial has three markers: a circle on the left indicates the furnace is off; a dripping faucet in the middle is for hot water; a dripping faucet and three wavy parallel lines is for hot water *and* radiator heat. It's ninety degrees, and the dial is on the wavy lines.

"C'est marche?" I ask. It is works?

"Oui."

"J'ai l'eau chaude?" I have the hot water?

"Oui."

"C'est bon pour la d-d-douche?" a word I have trouble saying.

"Oui."

"Un moment."

I run into the house and turn the hot water on in the kitchen. YES! I run up the stairs to the first/second-floor bathroom and turn on the douche: YESS!! I run up to the attic and turn on that douche. YESSS!!! The water is hot and the spray is powerful. I'm delighted, and Donna will be, too. I go back to the shed and thank him. "Merci, merci, beaucoup. Tout est parfait." It's perfect.

"Non."

"No?"

"Non," and he shows me the function knob isn't working properly. When he turns the knob to hot water (the dripping faucet) the lights go off. It only works when turned to the radiator (wavy lines), which I think means using more fuel and more pressure, which I think means heavier use, which I think means more wear, and the ten-year warranty will last five years instead of twenty, not to mention that it's ninety degrees, and I don't need more heat. This is what I'm thinking, and chastising myself for not asking those warranty questions, when Monsieur C says, "Je téléphone a un ami, un expert. Il arrivera demain et le réparera."

The next day an old guy arrives in a rusty, beat-up jalopy, what I'd call a mechanic's car in the U.S., and is rare in clean and polished France. He has a Colonel Sanders beard and hair like Einstein's, meaning he's either very smart, or he's fried himself a couple of times too many—and he's smoking.

"Bonjour," I say, and shake his hand. His fingertips are mustard color, his nails lemon, his beard has banana-colored streaks, and his teeth are the color of corn.

"Bonjour," he says, shakes my hand, exhales a blast of smoke, and goes into the shed, inhaling, and smelling like *Tobacco Road*—the novel, not the golf course. There are five hundred liters of oil in the tank, paint, turpentine, gasoline in cans, and bottles of unidentifiable solvents, and he never stops smoking. I stay away from the shed as much as possible, wondering if my insurance will cover the damage from the explosion and who's paying for the expert—if he's part of the $10,000 cost or on top of it?

The next day, Monsieur C knocks on the door and indicates I should follow him to the shed. He points to the dial where the knob is still on the wavy lines.

"Cassé," he says. Broken.

I stand there, wondering if now is the time to ask about the warranty.

"Pas de problème," he says. "Ça marche." No problem. It works. And he shows me how: he walks through the house making sure all the radiators are off, lowers the pressure on the gauge, and leaves the knob pointing to the wavy lines. "C'est bon," he says. I know if I call Jean, he'll fix it. I also know if I call Jean, Monsieur C would be embarrassed. Rather than embarrass him, I live with a new, $10,000 furnace and broken knob.

The next day Monsieur C returns for a final check. The dial is on the wrong icon, where it's supposed to be, the burner is glowing, and all four green lights are glimmering. He goes into the house and turns the front hallway radiator on. Then he walks through the house and turns every radiator on—all nine of them—and goes back to the front hallway. He touches the radiator. It's cold. He walks through the house and touches every radiator. They're all cold. He makes one more circuit, and it's the same. He goes back to the shed and turns the knob on the pressure gauge. The needle goes up, then down. I don't know what this means, but Monsieur C does: there's a leak. There's no water on the floor anywhere in the house or the shed so the leak is underground—in the six feet between the shed and the house, or under my hundred-plus-year-old terra-cotta tile floor in my favorite two-fireplace, cathedral ceiling, granite wall living/dining room where the pipe enters the house. As much as I like heat, I don't want to destroy this floor. I'm going nuts thinking about my choices, but Monsieur C understands and has a solution. He takes me outside to show me.

He makes a digging motion and shows me where he'll dig up the area between the shed and the house. Then he makes drilling sounds and shows me where he will drill a hole through the three-foot-thick granite wall below ground level so when he covers the pipe with dirt the hole in the wall won't be seen. He takes me inside and shows me where the pipe will enter the room and run along the floor behind the couch, then up the wall—in the corner so it won't be conspicuous—along a twenty-foot wall, where he will drill another hole through another three-foot-thick granite wall and connect the new pipe to the old pipes that converge under the stairs and run through the house to the radiators. It's a project that involves digging, drilling, banging, and cementing; laying more than ninety feet of copper pipe and bending the pipe so it turns five corners without crimping; adding an air vent—like the second hole in a can of evaporated milk—so the water flows freely and consistently, and doesn't balk or dribble as it rises three floors—all of which he does by himself in two days.

The finished work is flawless, the copper piping perfectly bent, flush, fitted exactly into the corners and through the holes he drilled in the walls. The work is so perfect Jean admires it every time he visits, and the price is so fair and reasonable, I'm embarrassed to write it.

I now have hot water, radiator heat (turned off), and form-follows-function exposed copper pipes—my own private Pompidou—a new furnace with a ten-year warranty that will last five to twenty years, and Monsieur C, my friend and rescuer, who stops by regularly to visit me and the furnace to make sure we're both working and well. Often, he'll sit with me in the kitchen sipping coffee I make for him: two unshaven guys, one graying, the other dark, me talking crazy French, him repeating, "No problème, no problème," neither of us sure what the other is saying, nor caring. It's our time together that counts, and the time is always good. It's September, but when the time comes I want to be ready for winter.

La Martyre

Gloom. Yes, it happens even in France, Brittany, Finistère, Plobien. Sometimes the weather brings it on—a week or two or three of rain. Sometimes, the news: famine, murder, genocide, plague; xenophobia, racism, sexism, nationalism, any ism. Often it's personal: Donna's or friends' absence. Most often, though, it's existential malaise, and when that feeling/worry/concern becomes sentient and couples with bad writing or no writing, I'm glomed. Gloomed. Possessed by bleakness. It doesn't happen often, but often enough that I have strategies.

Sometimes, if the melancholia is weather inspired—it rains a lot here—I put on my jammies, get in bed, and read something funny: a chapter from *Catch-22*, *A Confederacy of Dunces*, *Pantagruel*, or *Candide*, for example, or watch anything Lubitsch or Marx Brothers on DVDs. Other times, I go to museums in Quimper, Brest, Pont-Aven, Morlaix, or Landerneau, and seek solace and inspiration in art. If it's sunny—as gloom is weather resistant—I go to the Pointe du Raz, Pointe du Van, and the rough Iroise Sea, the rhododendron and hydrangea gardens at Château de Trévarez, or the rocky ridges and wild heather and gorse moors of the Monts d'Arée and hope for revitalization and uplift from nature. And if the gloom is really deep and persists—like I've lost all purpose and hope—I go to the twelfth-century Daoulas Abbey, the thirteenth-century cathedral in Quimper, the sixteenth-century cathedral in Pleyben, or one of those magnificently restored Breton chapels.

Over the years, I've visited many such chapels—in Rumingol, Sizun, La Roche Maurice, Lampaul-Guimiliau, Saint-Thégonnec. They were in competition with each other when they were built in the fifteenth, sixteenth, and seventeenth centuries—tallest steeple, finest organ, greatest calvary, most sacred relics—and they're in competition with each other today: hottest heaters (for thin-blooded congregants); biggest pews (for longer legs, weaker backs, and wider butts); softest, most pliable floor coverings (for aging knees); brightest lights (for cataractic eyes); loudest sound system (for hard of hearing); and colorful pamphlets explaining the church's history in as many languages as possible—French, English, Italian, German, Spanish, and Japanese. These chapels are as much museums and cultural heritage sites as they are working churches. When I enter, I think, "My God, look what human beings can do." I go to them because they are illuminating and uplifting—and nothing like La Martyre.

La Martyre is squat, thick, dark, and heavy, weighted and folding in on itself—a house of horrors and sorrows. Forget the Passion, Redemption, Ecstasy, Rapture, and Eternal Life. La Martyre is about Death, Misery, Pain, and Suffering: the horrible things that happened to the saints to make them saints; the horrible things that happened to Jesus; and in case I forget (which I rarely do), the horrible things that will happen to me.

I go to La Martyre when the world is going to hell in a handbasket and I'm at my spiritual worst, feeling beyond repair, fearful that I am what I do, and nothing that I do or have done really matters. I go to La Martyre and feel worse—which after a while makes me feel better, because it's a spur, like failure, telling me the clock is running, and I'd better get going and do something, and sometimes afterward I do.

I drive into the village, and it's dead: the bar is closed; the hotel, Épicerie, Tourist Information. I park in front of the three-arched, twenty-foot-high, two-foot-thick granite wall that looks less like a triumphal arch and more like a barrier, separating *l'enclose*—the church, cemetery, and ossuary—from life and the living. Everything looks as it did the last time I was here years ago, only worse: more erosion, grime, cracks, stains, mold, breakage, loss, which I find comforting. It is, after all, why I'm here: to sink so I can rise.

I get out of the car and look up. Still there, above the wall, greeting the village and me, is the most basic of calvaries—a smaller-than-life-size Jesus and the two thieves being crucified. Jesus is in the middle, bigger and higher than the other two, and looks sad—I know how he feels—one of a long line of Jewish boys who became a martyr trying to please His mom and dad. The guys next to him look worse. Except for different knees bent, the one to His left, the bad guy, looks just like the guy on His right, the good guy. It's hard to tell who won and who lost. Jesus Himself looks spacey, gazing down at a tiny pietà on the arch below Him—at His dead self in His mother's lap—as if thinking, "What am I doing here, and how long will this last?" Two questions I often ask myself.

I step up the three steps and over the two-foot-high slab of granite placed across the top step to block Death's entry, which is odd, because as far as I can see, Death is already in. The courtyard itself is a cemetery.

I walk around several tombstones and stop in front of the chapel. The main portal leans to the right, looking like the entry to a cartoon haunted house—except this house isn't funny. Arched around the doorway is what once was a halo of granite bishops, saints, apostles, and angels, and now—I count them—are sixteen vacant pedestals and more than a dozen worn, stained, cracked, and ravaged heads, faces, and torsos. It's a deconstruction site if I ever saw one. There ought to be an "Enter at your own risk" warning, or something that says, "Hard hats won't help!" "Damned if you do, damned if you don't." There's been zero attempt to clean, restore, or enlighten anything. Basically, life happens, and this is all you need: a chapel, an ossuary, and a cemetery.

I enter the porch and am greeted by Ankou: an eighteen-inch granite statue of a merciless, wrathful skeleton holding a child's severed head under his arm as if it's a gift he's been saving for me. *Bienvenue.* Welcome! Makes a fellow feel right at home—which to them I guess it is, because this is where we're all going. If I have any doubts, there's a carved angel on the holy water font with the Breton words (translated by *Lonely Planet*), "Thou shall remember my judgment—such will be thine—Today it is for me, tomorrow is for thee!" And if I still don't get it, another statement cuts to the chase: "I kill you all." That's the entrance, and still I enter. It's been that kind of week.

I step into the darkness, waiting for my eyes to adjust, but even in the twilight I see Him. Hanging from the crossbeam in the middle of the church, looking down, attending and ministering to His flock, is a wounded and bleeding larger-than-life-size Jesus. I follow His gaze to a tiny wooden skull and bones ten inches below his nailed feet. He's staring at Death, not victorious or confident or gloating, just looking, taking it in, and wondering like the rest of us, "How did this happen to me?"

I walk into the nave, set with its de rigueur uncomfortable wooden chairs with their high straight backs and impossibly short legs and narrow, narrow seats, too narrow for even a bony ass—and Breton people aren't built like that. There's not a pillow or cushion in sight. Or source of heat. Or kneeling bar to keep you off the hard, cold floor. It's the kind of place that lets you know you don't matter, you're nothing, temporary, and shouldn't expect too much, because this is the way it is and all you're going to get.

The windows and altars tell the story: temptation and punishment, greed and punishment, selfishness and punishment, doing good and punishment; betrayal, capture, misery, pain, agony, judgment, and death. And if I still haven't gotten the point, there's the ossuary next door, the cemetery surrounding the chapel, and the ubiquitous memorial listing the names of the dead from World Wars I and II to remind me the line between here and there is short and straight and connected.

The ceiling is blank, unpainted and unvarnished wooden slats—no stars, moon, sky, angels, or heavenly peace. The string and hammer beams are carved with pastoral scenes, scenes from the life of Jesus, and cornucopian abundance, each overseen and overshadowed by a beastie, monster, or viper. This is the chapel of a scared and superstitious people, people close to nature and afraid of nature, praying to a God of vengeance, no forgiveness and no mistakes. God of I'm-gonna-get-you, no place to go and no place to hide, but Him and Jesus.

As I leave, I pick up a brochure (French only) and I'm astounded to read the name of the chapel is *not* La Martyre. La

Martyre is the name of the village; the chapel is Saint Salomon. Can this be? Can the scariest Breton chapel be named after a King of the Jews? No, I read. It's named after the Breton king who was killed—martyred—in this chapel and became a saint who was named after a King of the Jews. I find this comforting. Either Bretons are Jews of the heart, or Jews are Bretons of the heart—outsiders and victims, always expecting the worst and often getting it. And why not? Before all and after all, Jesus was a Jew.

I walk through the cemetery surrounding the church, noting people's ages on the tombstones and that most of them are younger than me, and stop in front of the ossuary to regard the carved head and torso of a triumphant-looking man holding a human skull in one hand and what looks like a femur in the other. Beneath him two angels hold banners written in Breton. One proclaims, "Death, judgment, freezing Hell. Think on that and fear it." The other, "Foolish is he who does not know he must die." Talk about truth in advertising!

On the drive home, I think about life in the U.S. and how we're bombarded by death—death by disease, mayhem, bacteria, poverty, bridges collapsing, cars colliding, forest fires, gas mains bursting, drought, earthquakes, hurricanes, guns, drugs, suicide, smoking, viruses. Every day on TV, the radio, internet, the press, Death arrives in a million different ways, and every time it's new, a surprise, an outlier, unexpected, undeserved, alien, and always, always too soon. In France, Death is on your plate and next door. A fish on your plate looks like a fish, with its head, tail, and eyes; a bunny is a bunny, you can see it in the *boucherie*; a chicken has feet and a neck when you buy it. Whole pigs—from tail to snout—roast on spits. Kids have pets—bunnies, chickies, goats, sheep, *horses* that suddenly disappear. Abattoirs advertise. People die in their beds in their homes—and they're buried in their village cemeteries, which are in the middle of town, next to the church—unlike the U.S., where cemeteries are often removed, hidden, farmed out, *impersonal*—cities of the dead in the middle of nowhere. In Brittany, houses are built from the same stone as tombstones, and sometimes even with tombstones.

Clearly, these are a people accustomed to death. How could it be otherwise? They're Catholics, farmers, and fishermen: death, death, and death, not to mention all those war memorials in every village and two thousand years of being invaded—by Vikings, Celts, Carthaginians, Franks, Romans, including Julius Caesar himself, and in every century between the eleventh and twentieth by the Anglo-Saxon Brits. The reminders are everywhere: Roman ruins, medieval fortresses, Louis XIV Vauban forts, Napoleon's prisons, Nazi bunkers. Even now, nuclear submarines and the French navy are based in Brest and Lorient. This little piece of coastline controls the North Atlantic and the North Sea and over time everyone has wanted it. Otherwise, it's peaceful.

It's part of the contradiction and absurdity of everyday life. Long, sandy beaches, warm, inviting, emerald-green seas, heather in the hills and on the cliffs, rainbows and sand dunes, huge blue skies with cotton-candy clouds, all punctuated with indestructible cement bunkers complete with underground tunnels and gun turrets. You cannot go anywhere and not be struck by the beauty—sky, land, light, flowers—and the smell of death: pigs, chickens, German bunkers, war; the starkness of the stone houses softened by geraniums and hydrangeas adorning them.

When Monsieur P goes to the hospital for his annual tests, I ask when he's going to return. Madame shrugs, "Never. Who knows? It's out of our hands. Expect the worst," and Monsieur says, "Mardi." Tuesday. That's the range: from the apocalyptic to the ordinary. Back and forth, forth and back, a dichotomy and motion I'm used to, but there's something about this place—La Martyre, Brittany, France—that makes time seem longer and shorter, like the slowness at the start of a journey and the speed at which we go home.

Editing (not quite) . . .

Every year, I resist doing U.S. work in France because I have plenty of French work to do—like making sure the beach is still there in the daytime and Venus and the Milky Way are out at night, eating oysters and crêpes, drinking cider, and thinking about getting my front gate fixed. It's my down time, which is my up time, and I don't want to spend it working. So when Marie, the bright, young editor of my second book about living in France, sends me an email saying she's leaving the publisher to go back to school to get her doctorate in literature, and *(not quite) Mastering the Art of French Living* is her last project, and she wants to get started right away, I'm not happy. My first book, a collection of love and almost love stories, was edited from France, and the telephone bills were huge and many. The good news is that was in 1995—before Eric and Manu—and we won't be doing this editing by telephone. The bad news is we're doing it digitally, which Marie's ready for, and I'm ready for—thanks to Eric and Manu—but given my experience trying to pay my electric bill online, I'm pretty sure France isn't ready for.

I write her back Bartleby-style, saying, "I prefer not," and for emphasis add, "I have lots of important things to do."

"I understand," she agrees, and attaches the first thirty pages of the manuscript in a Word file, adding, "August 3 is my last day." It's June 30 when I receive this. I know, because it's the day my problems begin.

Most writers would simply open the file and begin—but not me, and definitely not me in France. When I edit, I want to see more than a paragraph or two at a time, which is all my laptop screen will show me. I want to see what comes before and after the section I'm editing, and I want to see it all at the same time, which means I have to see it on paper, which means I have to print it.

I open the file the next day to see what she's done—and what I'll need to do—and see red interspersed throughout the text and in the margin of almost every page, taking me back to Mrs. G's high school English class, a place I rarely wanted to be. If I were in the U.S., I'd print it out and start working. I *could* do the same in Plobien, because unlike almost everyone I know, I have a color printer, but it takes more than a minute to print a page in color—and there are three hundred pages in the manuscript, meaning it would take over five hours to print, but not five hours straight, like overnight while I'm sleeping, because this printer prints fifteen to twenty pages at a time, then stops for R & R, anywhere from minutes to an hour, depending on nothing, whim, or caprice. I'm lucky it doesn't need to go to Saint-Tropez to recuperate. . . . That's the first problem, and one I'd like to avoid.

I immediately begin searching for a French version of Copymat. There used to be a copy shop called Burocop two miles away in Loscoat, but it closed, probably because nobody could figure out what something called Burocop did. I search the internet and yellow pages and cannot find anything. I call Madame P, Sharon, Ella, Rick, and Monsieur Charles and no one knows of another copy place. The *poste* has a copy machine, but it doesn't have an automatic feeder and only copies one page at a time—at a cost of a euro ($1.15) a page. I call Gilles and Tatjana, who live in Brest, a city of 140,000 people, thirty miles away, and ask if they know a copy place, and amazingly they do, and even more amazingly, it's open the next day, a Sunday. Gilles says he'll go with me, "just in case," because he and I both know there's always a case with me. I go to bed relieved, sleeping the sleep of the fulfilled, until I wake early the next morning thinking about paper, which is my second problem.

In the U.S., printer paper is 8.5 x 11 inches. In France (and most of the rest of the world) it's 8.27 x 11.69 inches, meaning it's narrower and longer, meaning the manuscript will probably reformat when I print it, and the comments I make about line 1 on page 31 will actually be about line 25 on page 30.

I download the file to a flash drive, eat breakfast—because I know I'm going to need sustenance—and drive thirty miles to Brest, where Gilles takes me to an OfficeMax-size store in the heart of the city. I'm feeling good. Gilles is an international IT project manager and consultant and fluent in English, French, and Breton. There's nothing, I figure, he can't handle.

We enter the store on a mission. Gilles loads the flash drive on the computer and opens the file. The first thing I see is the manuscript *has* reformatted, and the content of each page has shifted. More problematic, Marie's edits have changed color— from a bright easy-to-spot red to an almost impossible-to-read pale yellow, not that it matters, because when we print five test pages none of her comments are there. The changes she made in the text are there (in pale yellow), but the margin comments—her explications, explanations, and questions—which are most important, are not. The computer or the printer or both can't read them or, worse, edited them out.

Gilles closes the file and goes online to access Marie's original Word file from my email, thinking/hoping it will work better than the copy on the flash drive. It doesn't. It's the same: a reformatted manuscript with pale yellow corrections I can barely see, and no visible margin comments—for 65 cents a page.

I decide to work from home, printing ten to fifteen pages at a time, and for the first week and thirty pages it works fine, except it's *very* slow, and not because of the printer.

Marie uses professional editing software that allows her to overwrite my punctuation and words, insert hers, and leave comments in the margin telling me why she did what she did and/or asking me the same. It's simple, efficient, and clear—and beyond me. Every time I use it, I don't overwrite, I erase and then spend minutes, which add up to hours, retyping what I originally wrote, what she changed, and what I want to say in response. After multiple failures, I go back to old school: I take her edited comments and changes from the reformatted file I'm using (there are at least a thousand) and locate them in the original unreformatted file she's using, and on a separate piece of paper, write, "Page 29, third paragraph, line two, okay;" "Page 72, last paragraph, line 5, please remove the comma and reinstate the dash." It's enough to make me miss the telephone.

She sends about thirty pages at a time. I go through them—colon by semicolon by dash by period, word by line by paragraph by page—and send responses back to her daily. There's a six-hour time difference, so we're never completely in sync—as her day begins, mine ends. Even so, we develop a schedule and routine that works—until my printer runs out of red ink. In the U.S., I'd have a replacement cartridge in my drawer. I don't have one here because I rarely print in color, and I've never run out of ink. I'd continue in black if I could, but I can't: the printer won't work if there's an empty or missing cartridge. In the U.S., I'd go to the real OfficeMax and resume printing with a new cartridge in less than an hour. In France, it takes five days: first, Eric and Manu have to order it from God-knows-where; second, it has to be delivered by God-knows-who, what, and how; third, it's Friday, the order won't go in until Saturday, and the store is closed Sunday and Monday, so I get it on Tuesday, five days later, which slows me down even more.

By August third, we've completed a third of the manuscript, and in the next three months, while she's in school at Ithaca, and I'm in California, we finish the rest. Some writers, I know, hate their editors—but not me. I love Marie: she's made my book a better book. In return, I give her a well-deserved two-week vacation in Plobien. I want her to see and experience the beauty of everything she's read about directly, and if, by chance, she returns to publishing and is the editor of my next book, I want her to know why I plan to edit it in the U.S.

In the U.S., I do. In France, I am . . . at the beach, with friends, eating oysters and crêpes, drinking cider, thinking about fixing my front gate, and all I want—all I ever wanted—now more than ever—is to be, to be, to be. . . .

The Wedding of Tanguy and Emilie

Donna and I are going to our first French wedding. My friends Bob and Loni's daughter, Karen, had an American wedding in France, but this is a *vrai* French wedding—civil *and* church—the whole shebang.

We've been invited to other weddings, but missed them because we were in California, and once because I had the wrong village. I thought it was in Montauban in Brittany, near Rennes, three hours away, not Montauban in the Tarn, nine hours away, and too far to go when I discovered it the day before the fête. This time, though, I'm confident—as confident as I can be in France—that I've got it right, and I feel that way until the day I see Bruno and Gérard dressed to the nines, tens, and twelves, and then I don't.

Bruno wears shorts all summer—as far as I can see the same shorts. If he must wear pants—like at work—he wears Dockers, though I suspect there are days he wears his doctor's gown over his shorts. I've never seen a French person—a professional!—who cares so little about dress or appearance. Gérard, too. He's a cattle rancher with a herd of three hundred Charolais cows, the best beef in France. He always wears jeans and cowboy boots, work jeans for the beef, pressed jeans for the rest of his life. I've known Bruno and Gérard for years, traveled with them, gone to restaurants and parties with them, stayed at their homes, and never, ever, have I seen either of them wear anything but the most casual clothes, and then, here, on the two-lane country road in front of my house—at two o'clock on a hot Saturday afternoon—they're going to a friend's daughter's wedding dressed like the beaus of the ball: Bruno in a black suit, white shirt, black bow tie, and straw hat—*a boater!* Gérard in a fitted—looks bespoke—brown suit, white shirt, and tie. They are dapper, dapper, dapper—which means trouble for me: the clothes I plan to wear to Tanguy and Emilie's wedding look nothing like theirs.

A week later, Donna and I are apéritifing with Bruno and Françoise on their terrace. "Une moment," I say, and walk back to our house and return in my full dress-up regalia—what I wear in the U.S. to weddings, funerals, sit-down birthday dinners, and retirement parties: polished black shoes, black socks, black slacks, a mauve shirt, and a charcoal gray vest with thin white pinstripes, à la Eliot Ness, holding my "in case of emergency" hand-painted, rainbow-colored silk tie in my hand.

"Oh la la," Françoise says.

"Beau," Bruno says.

Donna says nothing.

"Merci, merci, merci," I say, smiling, relieved. "C'est bon pour le marriage?"

"Non," they all say in unision. The verdict is unanimous. I look fine, handsome, beau—*and* I need a jacket, which is what

Donna told me in California, and why she's been quiet until now.

For Bruno, it's over. He's given his verdict, and that's all he's going to do. Except for wine and food, he hates shopping. Everything else is Françoise's bailiwick, which is why a few weeks later she takes Donna and me jacket shopping, something I dislike doing in the U.S. and suspect I'll dislike even more in France.

In the U.S., I go to Macy's or the Men's Wearhouse and buy something sedate, conservative, and classic—a navy blazer or Harris tweed—that I won't have to replace for a decade or longer if I'm lucky and don't spread, shrink, or spill. In France, I go to Leclerc *supermarché* and the Armor Lux clothing outlet store for *troisième marquage* sales. But not today. Today, I'm going where Françoise takes me. I've had three suits in my life, one for my bar mitzvah and one for each marriage, each one worn once, and I don't want another. That leaves sport coats, which is a problem. French men wear bright red, green, blue, yellow, and weirdly colored plaid jackets; jackets that are form-fitting-tight, too short, with wide lapels, narrow lapels, or no lapels; too many buttons or not enough buttons; cut pockets, uncut pockets, no pockets—nothing I'd even try on, which is why two hours and five shops later, I'm still jacketless and ready to quit. Looking uncourant can be fashionable in its own independent antihero Jean-Paul Belmondo–ish way, but looking like a clown is looking like a clown. I don't have much choice about being a fool, but a clown, *non*. I won't do it.

"Un de plus," Françoise says, and drives to a shop in a mall that has the same selection as the others: boring suits and unwearable phosphorescent sport coats. Those are my choices. I'm ready to leave, but Donna and Françoise have begun shopping, so I roam the third, fourth, and fifth racks and find what apparently no *Façonnable* French man would wear: a silvery-gray, twill, two-button, lightweight, normal-size lapel, cover most of my ass, western-fitted sport coat that's been marked down—*troisième marquage*—three times. I put it on, and from across the shop, Françoise, who rarely speaks English, yells, "*Yes!*" I look in the mirror: it fits and will look good with my black slacks, mauve shirt, and "in case of emergency" tie, which I now guess I'll be wearing. Sixty years ago, in high school, I wore white dress shirts, skinny black ties, and brightly colored Frankie Avalon horizontally striped cardigan sweaters and was voted *second*-best dressed in my class. Now, all I want is not to be worst dressed. Such is how my world turns.

I buy the jacket, and Donna, who has packed several wedding outfits and pairs of shoes (and paid extra for baggage) so she has choices—depending on her mood, the weather, what others are wearing, and not wearing—buys two more outfits.

One more thing remains to be done. Weeks before, I received an email from one of the wedding planners about something called *la boulette*. I looked it up and saw it means ball or blunder or dumpling, none of which seemed immediately important, though I was a little concerned about blunder. I had enough to worry about with my electric bill, bees, and what to wear to the wedding, so I set it aside—until now, two weeks before the wedding, and ask Françoise, "Qu'est-ce que c'est *la boulette*?"

She explains, but neither Donna nor I understand. She pantomimes writing, then rolling her hands together as if making a meatball or snowball, and underhanded tossing it away. She repeats this several times, and we still don't get it: it doesn't snow here, no one plays baseball, and no one would throw a meatball—*or dumpling!*—away.

She turns on her laptop and shows us: *la boulette* is a wedding game, like pass-it-on. You write a message to the newlyweds on a piece of paper—some advice or warning, hope, prayer, joke, or prophecy, then scrunch the paper into a ball—a dumpling?—or I guess if you write the wrong thing a blunder, and drop the ball on the ground. Then, with someone videoing you, you reach to your left, pick up your scrunched ball/blunder/dumpling, unscrunch it and hold it up so the message can be read, then you rescrunch it and toss the ball/blunder/ dumpling to your right. Each guest is invited to send a video—hence the email—that will be linked to other videos so it looks like one constantly changing message passed from the first sender to the last. The result is a three-or four-minute non sequitur *I Ching* message passed to the newlyweds. Our message is Ouiiiiiiii—pronounced Weeeeee—a French-English pun we're proud of. Françoise videos us with her phone and sends it to the wedding planner.

Ball/blunder/dumpling sent, a contribution to Tanguy and Emilie's next travel adventure in a gift envelope, enough clothes for a week, and we're off. We're going to Le Château de la Plinguetière for a two-day destination wedding, five and a half hours away, on the other side of the Loire, near Nantes . . . .

I drive past the open gates onto a long driveway and circle a late-nineteenth-century two-story brick-and-cut-stone Georgian manor house, passing well-disciplined gardens, a wooded park, outbuildings, statuary, and lots of individual cabins with private decks. I'm searching for the entrance, which turns out to be a tiny service door in the rear, not the grand front door I tried and failed to yank off its hinges.

Donna waits in the car like the cavalry while I go inside to register.

"Bonjour," I say to the youngish woman sitting behind a desk in a sparse modern room that looks like a vestibule. "Je suis ici pour le marriage Tanguy et Emilie."

"Bonjour," she says. "Votre nom?"

I know the answer, and I also know knowing the answer is one thing, and answering correctly is another. "Monsieur Greenseed," I say.

"Bienvenue." She nods, checks me off a list, and hands me a map of the grounds with directions to our room, which is in something called Le Bâtiment les Oiseaux, the Birds House.

"Merci," I say, turn around, and walk into Catherine, Georges and Yvonne's daughter, Gilles's sister, and Tanguy's mom, whom I first met almost thirty years ago when she visited me with her father and told me I needed to cut my trees.

"Bon-jour! Fé-lic-it-a-tions!" I sing, and give her a big California squeeze and four cheek kisses, which she returns with gusto. Everything Catherine does is with gusto. She's the most Italian French person I know. Olivier, her husband, is the most energetic, making the Energizer Bunny look paralytic. Olivier never sits still. He flies. Literally: he hang glides. Once, he asked me if I wanted to fly with him, something I'd never even thought about doing, but now have on the top of my no-go list along with bungee jumping, riding the Cyclone, and a third prostate biopsy.

"Dinner in Nantes tonight," she says, and goes to greet new arrivals.

Donna and I go to our room in Le Bâtiment les Oiseaux, which really is like a birdhouse, a *pigeonnier*, a dormitory with multiple roosts, and, to my dismay, a shared shower and toilet far,

far away, down a long hallway, in what for a seventy-five-year-old with an at-least-once-a-night usually around 2:00 a.m. get-up-to-pee routine, could be in another galaxy. It reminds me of St. Emilion when I got up at three in the morning to get some ice because my head was pounding from all the Médoc I drank at dinner and returned to the wrong room. Considering the hour and my insufficient attire the woman in the room was very understanding. That's what I'm thinking about, and wondering who our neighbors in the birdhouse will be and how they'll respond to an early morning visitor, when Donna says, "Remember St. Emilion?"

"I do," I say, and we laugh: she at what happened before, me at what could happen next, but thankfully doesn't. We return from dinner at 2:30 in the morning, time enough so my neighbors, albeit unbeknownst to them, don't have to worry about a night visitor . . .

I sleep well and wake, sweating. It's going to be a hot day, and I know from the invitation it's also going to be long: wedding at 2:30, *apéritif* at 5, dinner at 7:30, and *soirée* at 10:30. At our wedding, Donna and I were in bed by 11:30. I was fifty-three and she was forty-five. Tanguy and Emilie are in their thirties, late for France, but young for us.

I shower and wait for Donna. It's so hot, I'm perspiring by the time she returns. She tries one outfit after another and chooses the dress she bought with Françoise—sleeveless, below the knee, belted, lobster red with a white peony floral pattern that makes her look very Japanese even though everything she's wearing (except her earrings) is French: French dress, French sandals (Mephistos), French bracelet (Hermès, a birthday gift from Françoise and Bruno), French hair (done by Priska in Loscoat), and the pearl earrings I bought her in Japan after my mother shamed me into it. We were at Mikimoto, and I'd just bought Donna a necklace when my mother said, "Get her the earrings, too." I did, and she's wearing them and looks splendid. I'm wearing my wedding outfit sans vest: black slacks, black shoes, mauve shirt, new silver-gray, western-cut sport coat, and the hand-painted rainbow-colored silk tie Donna's dress designer made from a swatch of Donna's wedding dress. We stand next to each other, facing the full-length mirror, checking ourselves and each other out.

"Looking good," I say to Donna.

"Looking good," she says to me.

I know I'm telling the truth. I hope she is. Through the window, I see people getting into their cars. Most of the men are wearing dark suits (like Bruno and Gérard) and *pink!* bow ties (unlike Bruno and Gérard). Most of the women are wearing black, white, or off-white dresses, skirts, and blouses with matching heels. Everyone looks impeccable—except two scraggly guys without jackets.

We go out and join a long slow line of cars to the church, park on the grass with everyone else, and wait in another long slow line for a program and entrance. It's at least eighty-five degrees, ninety with the heat ricocheting off the cement sidewalk and stone church. I'm hoping we get seats near an open window or door, and we do—in the rear, near the door, behind a human mountain and its foothill. I can see lots of polished dark wood, varicose-veined marble, gold leaf, stained glass, statuary, a few Stations of the Cross, paintings of bishops and saints, and Him, but not the priest or the altar. I can hear, but it's French and Latin, so I don't understand.

I open the program—it's seven pages!—and see we're only at the welcome, *Accueil,* which is followed by the *Prière d'*

Ouverture, Liturgie de la Parole (first reading), *Psaume, Alléluia, Homélie, Sacrement du Marriage,* which includes (1) *Dialogue Initial,* (2) *Echange des Consentements,* (3) *Echange des Alliances,* (4) *Bénédiction Nuptiale,* more prayer, a *Bénédiction Finale, Chant d'Envoi,* which includes (1) *Chantez,* (2) *Priez,* (3) *Célébrez le Seigneur,* and *Remerciements* (thanks). No wonder most French couples eschew church weddings and opt for the fifteen-minute civil ceremony at the *Mairie* or the even quicker, living room or kitchen "I do" exchange of vows—especially in summer.

I'm thinking about this when someone closes the door. In the U.S., I'd take off my tie, maybe my jacket, too. Here, I suffer like everyone else. Well, not like everyone else—they're Catholic and French and *c'est la vie.* I'm Jewish and American and WTF. . . . A baby has the good sense to wail and complain, joined by another, and another, and another. I know from experience that French families are like the U.S. Marines, never wanting to leave one behind. It's part of their socialization process: teaching kids how to behave in public. In the U.S., parents spend fortunes *to* leave their kids behind, also part of the socialization process: letting them know life's more fun without them, and they'll pay anything to get away.

The babies wail louder, overriding the priest, till finally, amazingly, in every instance, the nearest male over the age of twelve lifts the kid and walks him or her around the perimeter of the church. *Inside.* For some reason, the kids are not taken outside, which is probably all they want, because the longer they stay inside the louder and longer they cry. They sound like a modern jazz quartet—The Contrapuntals—and one kid solos like a dissonant, dissident Coltrane, drilling all the high notes until Da Da Da Da blasts from the organ and startles her/him and me to attention.

Everyone (except the babies) stands and watches the door open and a très femme, très chic, seven- or eight-year-old Catherine Deneuve look-alike in a frilly white dress enters the church and parades down the aisle tossing handfuls of crimson rose petals, as at a coronation, which I guess in a way this is. She's followed by crimson-gowned bridesmaids, and—Holy moly!—Emilie. This is the first time I've seen her, and she's radiant: tall, lithe, tan, with a Palme d'Or smile, teeth, skin, and hair—a supermodel in her super gown on her super runway—catwalking to Tanguy, who's waiting for her at the altar (which I can now see). He's taller, tanner, maybe thinner—how do these French men do it?—in a three-piece dark blue suit, matching vest, and tie. He's beaming. She's beaming. Donna's beaming. If this was a musical, I'd break into song, Cole Porter, Irving Berlin, Lerner and Loewe, or Rodgers and Hammerstein, not Sondheim, who I usually prefer.

Forty-five minutes later, we're outside, mingling and gawking at people's accoutrements, as everyone (except the two guys without jackets) seems to be wearing something special and perfect for them: a tie, scarf, belt buckle, hat, earrings, brooch, necklace, garland—everything except a tiara—while Tanguy and Emilie make the rounds, "Bonjouring," "Merci-ing," shaking hands, and cheek-kissing everyone.

The closer they get, the taller I see they are. For Donna, at five-foot one, c'est normal. She's a shrimp. For me, it's disconcerting. One of the things I like best about being in France and Brittany is that at five foot seven and a half, I'm tall, and now, as I shake Tanguy's hand and stand on my toes to cheek-kiss Emilie, I'm reminded once again that I'm not. But I'm taller than the guy behind me who has to jump up and down to see Tanguy and Emilie fold themselves into a tiny two-seat red and black Austin-Healey convertible and drive away, waving and laughing.

The rest of us caravan back to Château de la Plinguetière to relax before the *vin d'honneur* begins in ninety minutes at Château de la Pigossière—or maybe it's the other way around. I don't know. The two Ps confuse me, especially since I can't pronounce either. I just hope I don't get tipsy or lost and have to ask for directions—but Tanguy and Emilie have already thought about that.

A bus—like a school bus—is waiting to take us from one Château P to the other, back and forth every thirty minutes, from 5:30 p.m. to 4:00 a.m. It's the best, easiest, and safest way to go, but it's not the American way, which mandates independence, freedom, flexibility, and wheels. Gilles, for his own French reasons, also drives.

I follow him, Tatjana, and their boys to another beautiful late-nineteenth-century two-story stone Georgian manor, where we're directed to a parking lot and a path that leads to the fête. The boys run ahead of us, excited—Emil to be with more adults, Ael, the older, to get away from them.

We follow the signs to the *cour intérieure*—the courtyard. I'm thinking patio, barbecue, a few plastic tables and chairs, and a bar. Ha! It's a park: hydrangeas, lavender, acres of greener-than-Augusta-National-Golf-Club lawn surrounded by more acres of old pine. Twenty-two acres, I find out later, about half the size of the Great Lawn in Central Park—and, like the Great Lawn on a hot summer day, crowded. Gilles, Tatjana, and the boys are immediately whisked away for family wedding photos. Donna and I stand there gaping at what looks to me like a party in a Fred Astaire movie before the dancing begins.

Beautiful people drift in and out of expanding concentric circles—like ripples in a pond—surrounding food tables and the bar, drinking, talking, and eating—three of the four most favorite activities in France. The smallest circle surrounds the cheese station, the biggest the oyster station, where bushels of seaweed-covered, dripping-wet oysters are shucked right in front of you. There's also a barbecue circle with seemingly limitless chunks of tender, marinated, skewered tri-tip; an open bar with unlimited wine, beer, whiskey, and pastis; a nuts circle—as in cashews, pistachios, and peanuts, not crazy uncles Jacques and Jean-Paul; and an endless conga line of mushroom, shrimp, pork, and chicken hors d'oeuvres bobbing by on trays.

Donna and I enter the oyster circle and make small talk—mine smaller than most, "C'est joli," "C'est magnifique," "J'aime beaucoup votre robe," hoping I said I like your dress, not I'd like to see you in a robe. I'm nodding, saying lots of "ouis" and "bien sûrs," speaking as little as possible. Donna is talking, listening, understanding, and responding. I walk away and stop to watch the changing kaleidoscopic iterations of family photos: cousins with the bride and groom, grandparents, grandchildren; Emilie's family, Tanguy's family, both families. . . .

"À table, à table," someone calls, and Donna, Gilles, and I walk to the salon. Behind us, a large group of people walks away.

"Why are they leaving?" I ask Gilles.

"They're not invited."

This is how I learn about the A group and the B group, which everyone in France, including the A and B groups, seems to know. The A group is invited to a sit-down dinner, the B group for *apéritif* and hors d'oeuvres. At the call for dinner—"*à table*"—the B group leaves and the A group sits. No wonder there was so much food—for the B group that was dinner. The B's leave full, happy, and sloshed. The A's, also full, happy, and sloshed, sit down for dinner. In the U.S, if you were in the B group, you'd feel shame. In France, it means you eat and drink more during the *vin d'honneur* to make up for what you're missing. For the A group, it means eating, drinking, and talking for two hours then sitting down and eating, drinking, and talking for another three, which will be followed by five hours of dancing, drinking, and eating.

We follow Gilles to a table where Tatjana is sitting with Gilles's older brother, Patrick (whom I've never met), Patrick's wife, two adult sons, and a baby. Donna and I introduce ourselves, four-cheek-kiss Tatjana, shake hands all around the table, including the baby's, and sit.

"Where are Ael and Emil?" I ask.

Gilles points out the window to another huge Augusta National lawn where groups of kids are playing ball games, board games, computer games, running, skipping, sitting, all of it supervised by paid professional staff, not a sulky teenage girl who was ordered there by her parents. In the church, where I expected respect, quiet, and decorum, kids were visible, present, and free to wail. At the party, they're silent, removed, and invisible. Clearly, French people have their priorities straight.

I pick up the menu to see what's for dinner, and—Oh my!— look at a photo of Emilie on a beach in a bikini, and she's every bit the supermodel she looked in her dress—and Tanguy is as thin as I thought. I turn the page quicker than I prefer. In the U.S., the menu would have a choice of steak, chicken, salmon, or some tofu-veggie thingie. Not in France. Here, there is no choice. Here, the *patron* knows what's best—and tofu-vegans don't exist or matter. Here, we're having *cannelloni de crabe*, *boeuf charolais,* and *chocolat et framboises,* but first we're having speeches, starting with Olivier's champagne toast.

I can't follow everything he says, but I can tell from the reaction—no back-slapping, raucous laughter, or flushed faces—it isn't a roast. I know from my fiftieth birthday party that French people are uncomfortable with roasts and don't like to be laughed at in public. In the U.S., ridicule is linked to ridiculous and is considered funny. In France, ridicule is linked to contempt and can end a relationship or start a war. Olivier's speech is French: warm, loving, sentimental, romantic, and nostalgic, and is followed by another from Emilie's dad, and by entertainment.

In the U.S., the bride and groom bask, and entertainment is provided by others. In France, the entertainment *is* Tanguy and Emilie. They're seated in chairs, back-to-back, and peppered with questions: who is the neatest? Who drives best? Who is fastest, slowest, smartest? It's the French version of the *Newlywed Game.* In the U.S., the TV couples disagree more than agree. They also compete, trying to outdo each other—often trying to make themselves or the other look foolish. Here, Emilie and Tanguy work together. There's no winner, loser, or prize. It's just fun—as it always is to laugh at other people's misconceptions of themselves and their partners, though with Emilie and Tanguy there aren't a lot, as they agree 90 percent of the time. Donna and I agree about 80 percent, and still argue about who's the better driver, because neither of us wants to admit who's the worst . . .

When the game ends, Tanguy and Emilie return to their table and dinner is served—and the *cannelloni de crabe* is every bit as tasty, creamy, and rich as it sounds, the *boeuf charolais*—the Wagyu of French beef—is every bit as marbled, and the *chocolat et framboises* is a mixed-media construction of colors, shapes, tastes, and textures.

Three hours later, at 11:00, after several bottles of wine and lots of conversation I don't understand—when everyone I know in the U.S. would be leaving or sleeping—tables are cleared and removed, chairs pushed against the walls, sparkling lights flash, and with no epileptic warnings, a glimmer ball spins, and the party begins.

Tanguy and Emilie start it off with a Lindy, working together even better than in the *Newlywed Game*. It's like *Dancing with the Stars*, and they are the stars. It's sexy and motivating, even for a non-dancer like me. I wait for a slow song, something I'm comfortable with, but apparently no one else is, as they western, swing, line, Lindy, and freestyle to Afro-hip-hop, rap, techno, French pop, and Anglo-American sixties rock, so I throw myself to the sharks and start my no-step-anti-rhythm routine, relieved to see no one is watching and no one cares, probably because they're all watching Olivier, who never stops moving, dancing with all of the women and half of the men, and Emil, Gilles and Tatjana's ten-year-old, who escapes the kids' group, joins the adults, and never leaves the dance floor. There's a line of women—like at a Sephora giveaway—waiting to dance with him. Ael, his older brother, stays with the older kids, not caring the least about the fête— except for the ice cream, chocolate, and macarons.

Periodically, the music stops so we can eat and drink *en groupe*, which French people prefer to eating alone, and there's more entertainment: there are the now universal videos of Emilie and Tanguy's childhoods, families, growing-up years, and growing-together years, including video of their travels—where they've been and where they want to go, letting us know what our gifts will be contributing to; there's *la boulette*, five minutes of funny, serious, and heartfelt messages strung together, but not ours because I waited too long and missed the deadline; there's a champagne fountain with waves of champagne tumbling over a pyramid of champagne glasses—and more toasts; a cake made from a painter's palette of dozens of pastel-colored macarons, and more chocolate, more ice cream, and more drink. At 2:00 a.m. a giant brioche—the size of a desk—is carried out and given to Emilie and Tanguy, who hold it aloft and dance all around the room for everyone to see, and then, like with everything else that's good in France, except the children, we eat it.

Sometime around three Donna and I drive back to Château P, and don't get lost. An hour later, the last bus returns with the last celebrants. It's a day and night Tanguy and Emilie will never forget—and neither will we—and our neighbors will remember it, too, and not for an early-morning invasion that never occurs.

I wake, thinking about food. I must be becoming more French. The invitation said brunch and entertainment starting at 11:30, but I'm dubious. Brunch is an American word, and in my experience French things with American names are horrific—like an American sandwich (baguette, ham, butter, lettuce, tomato, French fries, and a mystery white sauce); an American crime (mass shooting); and American business (closing all the branches and going digital). I'm lying in bed, thinking about passing on "brunch," but by eleven o'clock, I'm famished: the more I eat, the more I want to eat, even though the older I get, the less I eat at one time.

I get up to see what's happening, and see the Fred Astaire movie from the night before has segued into *Night of the Living*

Dead. Dozens of zombie-like people are roaming around looking for friends, family, and food. Others, looking *sportif* in body-hugging, eye-blinding, Day-Glo jerseys and shorts—having ridden fifty or one hundred or five hundred kilometers on their five-thousand-euro bikes—are also roaming around looking for friends, family, and food. Kids and toddlers are chewing on whatever they can. Dogs are doing what doggies do. One hundred and fifty people—I don't know how many dogs—are roaming the lawn, cabin porches, and parking lot—all of them hungry and waiting to eat.

I'm waiting, too, and brunch, it turns out—not surprisingly—is terrific, an all-you-can-eat French smorgasbord. . . . Tanguy, Emilie, Olivier, Catherine, and her mother, Yvonne, serve multiple ham products, multiple cheeses, made-to-order omelets, scrambles, sunny-side-up, easy over, not-so-easy-over eggs, and multiple, perfect, made-to-order savory and sweet crêpes. There are also multiple help-yourself wraps, yogurts, fruit, baguettes, *croissants*, *brioches*, *pain au chocolat*, *pain aux raisins*, butter, jam, milk, cream, coffee, tea, juice, and water, flat and sparkling. . . . If Napoleon had had these provisions, he would have conquered Moscow and changed the world.

When everyone has had their firsts, Olivier leaves the food line and becomes an impresario, volunteering three young men and women to entertain us. I don't know if they're couples, and it's not clear if they know, either, though it's France and everyone is exceedingly chummy. "Asseyez-vous, asseyez-vous," Olivier says, indicating the men should sit lotus-legged on the lawn and hands each one a hatchet and a four-inch-thick log. The first man to chop his log in half wins—Olivier doesn't say what, just wins—and for the men, like most men everywhere, that's enough. To make things interesting, he tells the men to remove their shoes and socks and instructs the women to blindfold "their" man with a swatch of black cloth he gives them. It's the women's job to direct the men where to chop: "À gauche," "À droite," "À droite," "Encore."

In the U.S., a shoeless, sockless teenager blindly swinging a hatchet would bring out insurance forms, permission slips, waivers, doctors, lawyers, EMTs, and cops. In France, it's entertainment. As the blind men wait for the game to start, Olivier places one sock from each man on the log in front of him. *This* is the game: chop-a-sock. The first man to shred his sock wins. People are curious enough to stop eating—itself a miracle in France—and cheer their favorite Jean-Paul Bunyan to victory.

"Un, deux, trois," they begin. The men chop, the crowd cheers. The women furiously yell directions . . . "À gauche," "À gauche," "À droite . . ." and tattered pieces of cotton, wool, and polyester land on bystanders' heads and shoulders like dandruff.

"Fini," Olivier calls. "Terminé."

The men remove their blindfolds to see who won and are startled to see their used-to-be, hopefully not-favorite socks sliced, diced, and shredded. The winner is given a new pair that doesn't look as good or expensive as his old pair. The other two walk away barefoot. If it were me—loser *or* winner—I wouldn't be happy, but these guys and girls seem pleased to have been chosen to serve.

Meanwhile, Emilie, Tanguy, Catherine, and Yvonne have packed bags of food in cardboard containers, along with napkins, plastic utensils, and soft drinks for each family to take home, and we begin the process of leaving. French people—at least those who like each other—abhor goodbyes, and prolong them with lots of *au revoirs, à bientôts, merci beaucoups, á la prochaine fois*, California hugs, handshakes, and cheek kisses, all of which we give and receive repeatedly. Then we take our bag and leave in time to get home to open it and eat.

We're already looking forward to next year. Tanguy's brother, Paul, and his longtime girlfriend, Elise, are getting married, and Donna and I are invited. I already have my jacket and a year to find a non-pink bowtie and figure out how to tie the knot. It doesn't get much better than that: purpose, direction, and an achievable goal for me; another opportunity to shop for clothes for Donna—but the weekend of the wedding we're at a book fair in Budapest because my book *(not quite) Mastering the Art of French Living* was translated and published in Hungary, and the year after that is COVID-19—and for the second time in twenty-nine years, I'm not in Plobien, and the absence is a hole in my life.

Loni and Bob and Me

I'm thinking about Bob and Loni. We met on the ferry going from Le Conquet, the westernmost part of mainland France, to Ouessant, the westernmost island in France, the first summer after I bought my house.

It was a gorgeous, sunny, calm day. I know, because I would not have been there otherwise. The sea between Le Conquet and Ouessant is notoriously, dangerously rough, and there are hundreds of sunken ships and drowned sailors to prove it. There's even a Breton saying about approaching Ouessant and its sister isle, Molène: if you see Molène, you're in trouble; if you see Ouessant, you're too late. Strong currents, gigantic tides, nasty fog, changing winds, and a ship-eating coastline of sea-covered rocks and buried sand drifts make Ouessant a deathbed—and explain why the D-Day landings were on the Normandy beaches and not in Brittany, and why I'm certain it was a calm and gorgeous day.

I was wearing my Oakland A's sweatshirt, holding the railing and searching the sky for cloud formations and the quick, out-of-nowhere weather changes Brittany is famous for, when an older, shorter, tanned, crop-haired, muscular guy wearing gray cargo shorts, beat-up Birkenstocks, and a striped green, orange, and white long-sleeved soccer shirt came over to me and asked, "American?"

"Yes," I say.

He says, "Bob." And that's how we meet.

He introduces me to Sunny, their golden retriever who always travels with them, who's sitting next to him, wagging his tail and happy to meet me, and to Loni, his wife, who is not as effusive as Sunny, but also happy to meet me and to have someone for Bob to talk to because, as I later discover, Bob is the talkative one in their marriage, the easygoing outgoing one who meets new people. He gets great pleasure in meeting them, bringing them together, and bringing them home. Loni, more purposeful, is the planner and practical one, like, okay, now that we've brought them together what do we feed them, and what do we do about Monsieur A, who definitely won't like Monsieur B? Bob is the one who engages. Loni is the one who sees obstacles and tries to control them, like when Bob is driving, Loni often screams, "Watch out!" Happily, luckily, Bob moved toward me that day on the ferry, and Loni didn't scream, "Watch out!"

She goes back to reading her guidebook about Ouessant and where they should have lunch while Bob and I continue to chat and discover things we have in common: home (San Francisco Bay Area), politics (anti-Bush and Gulf War I), prose (Vonnegut and Shakespeare), sports (Giants, A's, Warriors, and Niners). It's their third trip to Brittany, my second—the first year after my girlfriend and I rented the house and two years before Donna arrives. They're in Brittany to attend the huge (tens of thousands of people) annual Celtic festivals in

Lorient, Vannes, and Quimper, for the music, dance, costume, art, food, theater, and historical re-creations even though neither of them is Celtic or speaks French. "I'm here," I tell him, "because I have a house in Brittany."

Loni puts her book down and says, "Really? We've been thinking about buying," and asks me how, when, where, what, and how much. I tell her, making everything sound fun, funny, and easy, forgetting I had Madame P on my side, and that it was heart-thumping, sleep-depriving, knuckle-biting frightening at the time. Afterward, I feel guilty for understating the challenges and maybe getting them in over their heads—but that's before I know Loni and that she recently made a killing and retired early by selling California's largest H&R Block branch for more money than I can fathom—and over the years I've tried.

I now know there's not much she can't do when she puts her mind to it (except learn French) and nothing she can't purchase when she wants to—which is why the following year they have their house on the Île aux Moines (the Island of Monks), ninety minutes south of Plobien, in the Golfe de Morbihan, where there's lots more money and sun.

The Île is famous for oysters, movie stars, and rich Parisians. Think the Hamptons, Fire Island, Cape Cod, and Kennebunkport: no cars, Red Flyer–like wagons, lots of boats and beaches, a botanical garden variety of flora, and scores of majestic two- and three-story stone houses. Their two-story house touches the Golfe. Water licks the foundation at high tide. At low tide, they have a semi-private beach. It's every bit as perfect and idyllic as it sounds: a secluded house on a beautiful, almost private island, where everything except oysters, seafood, and potatoes are imported, and nothing is easy, cheap, or convenient, which is why I think we went wine shopping and also why Bob bought a boat.

I don't know if it's Loni, the planner and bursar, or Bob, Captain Social, or both of them together, but early one Saturday morning when I'm visiting we ferry to the mainland to get their car and go wine shopping. The good news is their car is close to the ferry in a garage that came with the house. The bad news is the garage was built for a Mini, and they lease a four-door, high-end, luxury Peugeot that by the end of every summer is a little less luxurious, and at the end of one summer was a little shorter, too.

Bob backs out of the garage with Loni's help—"Left, left, right, watch out!" They've been here about a month, and the car already has a long scratch and a dent, which, given the garage and Bob's driving, is a miracle. That I voluntarily get in the car and sit in the back seat is another . . .

Bob drives south, toward Nantes, Angers, and Loire wines with Loni periodically screaming, "Watch out! Don't hit [fill in the blank]." An hour and a half later, she points and says, "There it is," and Bob turns onto a narrow, cracked, and bumpy dirt road leading to a winery and parks as close to the *cave* as possible without hitting it.

It's 10:30, and we line up for a tasting, which also happens to be our breakfasts. It doesn't take long before we're looped. After about a dozen "tastes" and lots of discussion, Bob and Loni select the wines they want—one white and one red—and we stagger back to the car with the wine guy following us, pulling a hose like he's at a gas station, and begins filling a half dozen squished twenty-liter—five-gallon—plastic containers Bob has tossed on the ground.

He fills half with white, changes hoses, and fills the other half with red. With each filled container, everyone gets happier and happier. The vintner is happy, with euro signs in his eyes. Bob is happy having enough red and white for the rest of the summer. Loni is happy nothing's gone wrong, and I'm happy to be there. I've never seen anything like it: a wine filling station. It gives a whole new meaning to the phrase "top it off."

"What's this called?" I ask.

"Vrac," Bob says.

"What?"

"Vrac. Bulk wine."

Later, I look it up. There are thirteen English meanings of VRAC, including Virtual Reality Application Center and Volume Regulated Anion Channel, and three French: bulk, loose, and higgledy-piggledy, none of which make me thirsty enough to want to drink it.

Bob drives back as if we're hauling nitroglycerin, with Loni pointing out various things for him not to hit. I have no memory of how we—or they—got the containers from the car to the ferry (about a quarter mile) or from the ferry to their house (about one mile), which means I wasn't there, or it was so terrible I've blocked the memory. I do remember funnel-filling dozens of empty wine bottles with vrac and corking them with an ancient corking machine Bob found in the *cave* under their house. It was the discovery of the corker and the zillions of empties the previous owner left that are the reason—or excuse—for the search for vrac.

I did this once, but Bob and Loni did it every year for years. All I can say is if you start drinking at noon—as we often did—by dinner time vrac's not too bad. It's also why whenever I visit them I bring two or three mature bottles of red—bottles with labels—as a gift for them, but also for Donna and me.

After the vrac discovery, Bob and Loni never have to worry about running out of wine and making last-minute shopping trips again, which is saying something, because Bob is very social, and Loni is very gracious, and both of them are very generous, and the wine flows higgledy-piggledy on the Île aux Moines.

It was when Bob got his boat, though, that transport really became interesting. For one thing, it provided many more things for him to hit—and unlike a car or a gun or many other lethal things, no license, permit, training, knowledge, skill, aptitude, or ability are required to buy, own, or use one.

Bob wanted a boat ever since they bought their house. After all, they live on an island in a house touching the Golfe, and most of their friends, including their best friends Gilles and Sandy, have boats, so why shouldn't he? A private stone dock attached to their terrace made docking simple and easy, but it was built by the previous owner without a permit and is illegal for Bob to use. That could have deterred him—but most people who have boats on the Île don't have their own dock. They tie their boat to a buoy in the Golfe and dinghy their way to shore, which is what Bob would have to do, too—except most people don't have the Golfe lapping their house at high tide, which means *they* can leave their dinghies on the shore and find them when they return, and Bob can't. He has to Rube Goldberg a contraption to pull his dinghy in and tie it to the house so it won't float away. Still, it's a small price to pay for the joy and pleasure of having a boat, and Bob pays it, buying a small motorboat and dinghy.

A few weeks later, Donna and I visit, and Bob surprises us by meeting us at the ferry dock in his new boat, grinning.

"Where's Loni?" I ask.

"Making lunch."

"Uh huh," I say, suspicious.

It's sunny, windless, cloudless, calm—the only kind of day I want to be in a boat—so I step in. Donna jumps in after me, and Bob—happy, tan, captain of his ship (I hope)—turns the boat around and motors toward their house, a direct ten-minute run across the channel, passing other boats and captains, waving.

I'm impressed. Bob *is* the captain of his ship, master of his fate, so obviously, contagiously pleased with himself, his life, and command that I relax. I, who do not swim, who on land as well as in water try to live by the dictum, "Don't get in over your head," am in waaaaaay over my head and thrilled about it. Normally, we'd be on the ferry, crowded with dozens of people, kilos of cargo, three meters above the sea. In Bob's little boat, we're part of the sea: I smell it, feel the spray on my face, the gentle rocking rhythm of the boat, lick salt from the fingers I dangle in the water. . .*This* is the kind of adventure I like . . .

Bob motors as close to the house as he can get, which is close, but because it's low tide, not close enough. Donna and I have to get off in the water, which ordinarily wouldn't make me happy—as in don't get in over your head—but there are no riptides, waves, or undertow, the water is glass-clear, about calf-high, and we're wearing flip-flops and shorts—and it's the only way off the boat. I lift our backpacks, which contain three bottles of Côte de Beaune, step into the water, and howl, "Yow!" It's ice.

Loni appears, wearing brown REI shorts and a yellow T-shirt, smiling, waving, summer-freckled, tan, and greets us with "Bonjours" and "Bienvenues," hearty American hugs, French cheek kisses, and a table set for lunch. We sit and watch

Bob motor to the buoy, tie his boat, and dinghy to shore, where he spends the next thirty minutes Rube-Goldberging the dinghy to the house. When he finishes he joins us, and Loni serves lunch.

Weeks before, they bought an entire Parma ham, and since then it's been Parma everything. They eat it daily (we discover) and share it with everyone who comes to their house. Lunch is Parma and Cavaillon melon, langoustine salad, still warm *pain de campagne* with *fleur de sel* butter, and vrac. While we're eating dessert—fresh fruit compote with Loni's homemade orange sorbet—Bob says, "Let's go to Île-d'Arz."

None of us say anything, which says something, until Loni says, "I don't know, Bob. It's supposed to rain, maybe storm. We probably shouldn't go." A few more vracs, and it's "Why not?"—which is how, slightly looped, the four of us find ourselves on the boat.

It's sunny, windless, and calm; the sky is dotted with cotton balls; the sea eliding from jade to turquoise to opal. The fun adventure boat ride from the morning is fresh in my memory, and we're going very, very slowly—the speed I like best—past rows of oyster beds, careful not to make a wake and disturb them, or me, as we head out to sea.

Bob is exuberant. Loni is anxious. Donna looks for the life jackets and finds them under a seat. I look at the boats and ferries in the Golfe thinking they can probably save us if something goes wrong. For a while, nothing does—not until we're out of the channel, in the open sea, when Loni says, "Hurry, Bob, the storm's coming," and half the sky turns black.

Bob puts the boat at full throttle. I'm too scared to say anything. Years before, on a calm, sunny day in Madison, I went sailing with my college roommate, Earl, a storm came up, and every boat on the lake, including ours, capsized, and two people drowned. That's what I'm thinking about, feeling the wind nip, water chop, waves getting bigger, and the boat rock 'n' rolling as I put on my life jacket and buckle it tight. Donna and Loni look back, monitoring the storm. I look at Bob, who's reading a manual—hopefully in English, not French, as his French is worse than mine—trying to decide what to do as the boat goes waaaaay up then waaaaay down and thankfully not waaaay under. "Bob," Loni shouts, "watch out!" as we go up and down again and again—and between that and the rain we're soaked by the time we get to Arz. We dock and go to a *salon de thé* for *goûter* and wait for the storm to pass. Loni, Donna, and I enjoy pastries, ice cream, coffee, tea, and being alive as Bob recounts our adventure, concluding, "Pretty good for my first time out of the channel, don't you think?" None of us say what we think.

Later, back at their house, we eat a candlelit dinner on the veranda—vrac apéritif, melon and Parma, Loni's homemade fettuccine with fresh tomatoes, crevettes, bay leaves, and basil, two bottles of *our* red, mint-strawberry soup for dessert, and vrac digestif—and make up stories about the young couple on the pink, rocking catamaran we dub the "Love Boat" because the owner specializes in renting to honeymooners. We sit for hours, laughing, drinking, talking, as we only do in France, watching the winking lights on the passing boats, waiting for another fireworks sunset and its mirror-double on the Golfe, just another day and evening on the Île aux Moines.

I'm thinking about this because Bob just called me from France—a first. Usually he's loquacious, slow and circuitous in his speech, laid-back, and self-effacing, but not today. Today he was immediate and direct, and I knew there was trouble.

"Loni's been ill," he said. "She was misdiagnosed and went to the hospital for emergency surgery. Her appendix almost burst, and she got infected. She's okay, but she spent three weeks in the hospital in Vannes and she's shaken."

I could tell from his voice *he's* still shaken: a three-week hospital stay, the isolation and lack of medical care on the island, the length of time it took to get to the mainland, not having their own doctor, not having a second opinion, and, of course, not speaking French. They've had their share of medical issues: he's hurt his leg; she's hurt her back; there was the summer a nurse took the ferry from the mainland to give him a shot at the same time every day for several weeks, but this, this is a magnitude of a different order.

"We're coming back to San Francisco in a week," he said, "and thinking about selling the house and not returning to France," and now I am, too. Not immediately—they're several years older than me—but something I never thought about and couldn't imagine when I arrived in Plobien and began this journey thirty years ago is now in my head, and I wish it wasn't.

IV

—an unexpected breeze has sprung up, and we are moving again. But where are we being taken? Essex? The German Ocean? Or, if the wind is a northerly, then, perhaps, with luck, to France.
—Julian Barnes, *Levels of Life*

Looking Back

The first time I saw Paris I was twenty-one going on twenty-two. I'd just graduated from the University of Wisconsin in Madison with a bachelor's degree in history and was on my low-end, left-wing, grand European tour the summer before I started graduate school.

I cashed out my bar mitzvah bonds a year early and bought a $210 round-trip ticket on Northwest—an airline that, like so many other things I can recall, no longer exists. I was with a group of college friends, including the woman who two years later would become my wife—a marriage that officially lasted four years, but collapsed in less than two.

We arrived together, four women and three men, at Heathrow Airport, where we met the eighth, a woman who recently completed her junior year in Aix-en-Provence, the only one of us who spoke a semblance of French.

We explored London, then took the train to Dover and the ferry to Calais, and two by two hitched to Paris in pairs, not couples. I don't remember who I thumbed with, but I know I wore blue jeans, white T-shirts, and sandals, because that's what I wore then, and brought wheat jeans (to be au courant), blue jean cutoffs, a couple of sweatshirts that I wore inside out, a week's worth of underclothes, a dress shirt (by which I mean it had a collar, sleeves, and buttons down the front), a rain poncho, windbreaker, sleeping bag (flannel, not down), dress shoes, sneakers, and toiletries that I carried in a drab, olive green, canvas, steel frame, World War II military surplus backpack that sat on my hips and broke my back. I doubt I could even lift it today, let alone carry it for ten weeks across Europe.

Martin Luther King Jr. and Bobby Kennedy were alive. So were Elvis, Otis, Janis, Jim, Jimi, and John. De Gaulle was president of France again, and Mao was in his twenty-third year of dictating China, the Shah his twenty-fifth in Iran, and Franco his twenty-seventh in Spain. It was a year before *Sgt. Pepper* and *The Graduate*, Les Halles, Zola's belly of Paris, lived within the Paris city limits, and fewer than six thousand Americans were dead in Vietnam. . . . It was 1966. . . . It sounds unbelievable even to me . . .

So does this: twenty-one years after World War II, the tap water in France and Europe was unsafe to swallow, so I drank lots of beer, wine, and Coca-Cola; a typhoid shot and yellow proof of vaccination card were required to reenter the U.S. No card, no entrée. I carried that card and my first passport, a youth hostel card for cheap group dormitory sleeping bag nights, and a student ID for reduced fares. It was the last time you really could see Paris on ten dollars a day—and I did, by staying in a four-story walk-up.

Hotel rooms sans heat, sans water, sans bath, sans toilet, sans toilet paper, sometimes sans window, definitely sans housekeeping could be had for less than five dollars a night, and when the room was shared and the cost was split (with someone like a wife-to-be), along with the shower and towels that cost extra, the price of lodging was a gift for an American, a steal if you were French, and left more than enough—seven or eight dollars a day—for me to eat and do anything else I wanted, which was mostly sit in the Luxembourg and Tuileries Gardens (chairs cost), use the bathroom (toilets and hole-in-the-floor non-toilets cost), ride the Métro (second class), and visit museums and monuments (free or reduced price for students).

French men still wore berets and blue workman's uniforms and people pedaled whiny gas-powered Motobécane bikes, drove Citroën, 2CV *deux chevaux* cars, and began—or ended—each morning with a glass of red. Think Bresson and Doisneau! Public telephones and Laundromats were hard to find and, when found, were expensive. I cashed American Express traveler's checks (no credit cards) and bought francs (which no longer exist) at American Express offices and left notes for friends and received mail at Thomas Cook offices (which now exist only online). Television was not ubiquitous; neither were elevators, hot water, central heating, or indoor plumbing. Paris embodied authenticity, and I was enthralled—like when I listened to Édith Piaf and Billie Holiday or went to the Lower East Side. It was still more Henry Miller's and Louis-Ferdinand Céline's Paris than Macron's.

Buildings were dark, grimy, secretive, and mysterious, shrouded in decades of exhaust from cars and motorbikes, centuries of soot from wood and coal fires, and millennia of smoke from pipes, cigars, and gazillions of Gauloises and Gitanes cigarettes. I walked past and they'd smell of smoke, pee, bread, cheese, coffee, fish, and sweat, and even though I knew Haussmann had had his way with her less than a century before, Paris felt medieval to a kid from the New World.

Every night, a cluster of us would congregate at a restaurant in the Latin Quarter—a gaggle of geese at a pond, rabble to be roused?—and eat cheap student-fare Greek and Italian food, drink even cheaper Chianti and retsina, and recount our day's explorations, each person telling the others where s/he went, what s/he saw, and where the others should go. Sometimes, we traveled together, but mostly I traveled alone. I was on a very personal journey.

I tripped, mentally, sometimes physically, rambling cramped, cobbled, labyrinthine streets, ogling stone, wrought iron, mansard-roofed buildings; picnicked on baguettes, La vache qui rit cheese, and cheap red with friends and my wife-to-be in what seemed to me too closely cropped, neat, overly manicured seventeenth- and eighteenth-century imperial gardens; stood solemn and fluttery before monuments I'd only seen in movies and magazines: the Arc de Triomphe, Notre Dame, the Eiffel Tower, Shakespeare & Company, Sainte-Chapelle. . . . Paris was Adventureland, Frontierland, and Fantasyland all in one, none of it yet Disneyland, which was still twenty-six years away.

I strolled—a flaneur before I knew the word or what it meant, paying homage to the birthplaces of revolution and modernism, places I'd read about, studied, and imagined: Place de la Concorde, where the guillotine created equity; the Conciergerie, where Marie Antoinette lived her last days before being equalized; the Bastille, where the fire began; Versailles, where the spark was lit; *places* I wanted to see: Saint-Germain-des-Prés, Saint-Michel, Place des Vosges; Montmartre, Montparnasse, Sacré-Coeur, Père-Lachaise; Hemingway's apartment building, Victor Hugo's apartment, Henry Miller's Pigalle and Clichy, Nijinsky's and Diaghilev's

Théâtre du Châtelet. I was seeking, finding, and confirming my revolutionary and literary roots, fostering and feeding notions of myself as the political, literary, and social revolutionary I earnestly yearned to be. . . .

. . . on these streets, in this air, striding these cobbles, along that quay, avoiding that dog doo, drinking and eating in those bars and cafés, reading in that bookstore, Beckett, Joyce, Hemingway, Cummings, Fitzgerald, Gertrude and all the Steins; Picasso, Matisse, and Duchamp; Sartre, Camus, de Beauvoir, and the New Wave: Truffaut, Godard, Tati; Moreau, Deneuve, Seberg, Belmondo, and Bardot—Heroes of multiple revolutions!—and having read my Fanon, Marcuse, Pynchon, Heller, Robbe-Grillet, Debray, *New York Review of Books*, *Ramparts* magazine, and *Berkeley Barb*, I was ripe to join them. I thought the long arc of history and the future were ours—civil rights, anti-war, Cuba libre, Yeah, yeah, yeah, Eleanor Rigby, all you need is love. Who but Hannah Arendt, Richard Hofstadter, Joan Didion, and William Butler Yeats could have guessed what beast was coming?

The second time I saw Paris we both had changed—she was a lot cleaner, modern, and more expensive; I had a job, a suitcase, and a Visa card, though I still carried traveler's checks just in case. It was 1987, and I was there for a romance and a revolution of a different kind: the sexual revolution. It had already passed, lasting from 1963 (the pill) to 1983 (AIDS), but there was plenty of spillover, and I wanted to drink.

I was in an on-again, off-again relationship with a very attractive, very talented, successful (National Book Award finalist), ingénue-faced femme (for me) fatale, poet—precisely the kind of person an early-forties, barely published, unknown writer wants to be with in Paris, and—Voilà!—Freddie Laker and his ninety-nine-dollar-each-way People Express Airlines opened a branch in San Francisco.

I bought two round-trip tickets as a Christmas present, and a month later we flew from San Francisco to Brussels, landing at 4:00 a.m., the inconvenience, I'm sure, part of the reason for the convenient fare. We slept on the train to Paris and arrived in frigid, early-morning winter darkness to a deserted, chilly, semi-lit Gare du Nord just as the cafés were opening and setting up for the day. She chose one that looked like Colette had eaten there and we sat at a polished round table with a wicker basket full of warm, flaky croissants and chunks of crispy baguette, butter, and multiple jams that were waiting for us.

Her French was better than mine—*everyone's* French is better than mine—she ordered two *grandes cafés crèmes*, and we devoured everything, butter and all. Then, as people with jobs and places to go began arriving, and sunlight caromed off windows, mirrors, and the floor, we buttoned up and left, lugging our suitcases to the station's front doors, where, on the other side, through the glass whitely, all the way to the horizon, lay the longest, widest, whitest duvet of sparkling, shivering, glistening snow blanketing Paris: think Sisley winter white, Caillebotte urban, Utrillo quiet. I'll never forget it. It was the most romantic part of the trip.

We rode the Métro to the hotel I booked in the no-longer-belly of Paris new shlocky Les Halles area near the Pompidou Center. I was hoping for a night or three of Rabelaisian frolic, but it turned out to be one of our off-times, and Paris was more generous than she, as I'm sure it was also for her. We did lots of romance-y things—walked along the quays in moonlight, searched the booksellers for trove, rode the *bateau mouche*, kissed under the statue of Henri IV, held hands in the Tuileries and Luxembourg Gardens, ate and drank in dark, secluded, amorous wine bars, all without skipping a heartbeat. It would be another two years before she ended us, but this was surely the beginning of the end of the beginning. If you can't find Rabelais or even Masters and Johnson or Kinsey in Paris, where can you?

Four years later, in 1991, I returned to Paris with another very attractive, very talented, Central-Park-West-elegant poet, hoping for the romance I missed the last time. This time I was landing in Paris and going to Brittany, where she'd been before and wanted to return and show me its beauty. It was twice as good as the previous time I was there, and an eighth as good as I wanted.

That was thirty years ago when everything in my life was immediate, full of beginnings and bonjours. Now, it's more *à tout à l'heaure, à plus tard, à bientôt, à la prochaine, au revoir.*

Neighbors

My neighbor, François, died this year while I was in California. We never talked much—my failing more than his—and the last few years I rarely saw him, as he spent most of his time in his house and garden. His presence, though, was reassuring, and now that I'm in Plobien, I miss him more than I would have thought. Every time I drive in and out of my driveway I look over at his house, expecting to wave to him and call "Bonjour," expecting him to wave back and "Bonjour" me. I miss seeing him there, and I wonder who my new neighbor will be, and if s/he will be as careful, watchful, attentive, meticulous, and quiet as he.

I know a little about French inheritance laws—I'm learning more as I need to look into them for myself—and what I know is not reassuring. After I signed the *compromis de vente* (contract) to buy my house, I had to wait five months while the *Notaire* posted and searched—like marriage banns—for *any* heir who could/might/maybe make a claim of ownership and stop the sale. When I asked the same *Notaire* how the trust I spent two years and $2,500 creating in the U.S. would work in

France, he told me it wouldn't, that French law doesn't recognize American trusts. And I know this: a neighbor's house, two houses away, on the other side of Bruno and Françoise's house, sat vacant for twenty-seven years after the owner died, becoming a swamp in winter and jungle in summer, as the land was sometimes cleared and cleaned, and most often was not—and is why I'm very concerned about what happens to François's house.

In the U.S., inheritance laws are relatively simple: a donor with a sound mind, good imagination, and a better-than-average attorney can do almost anything s/he wants with his/her property, including keeping it for when s/he arises from a cryogenic sleep or the apocalypse—or leave it to a bird or a rat. Not in France. In France, there are zillions of rules for the living—parents must provide for their needy adult children; 35 percent of radio airtime has to be French-language songs—and zillions of rules for the dead.

In the good old days of the Henries, Louises, fore*fathers,* and primogeniture, life was structured and inheritance was simple: the oldest surviving son got it all, and Mom and the other children found themselves out to pasture. The revolution changed that for a decade, and all the children (but not Mom) got equal shares. Then, in 1804, Napoleon, a *second* son with a single, not very imaginative use for women (remember Josephine!) made a giant leap for men and menkind, who were not by definition kind men.

He bequeathed France, French territories, and the Europe he conquered his code—the Napoleonic Code, now known as the Civil Code—and hereditary rights and nepotism were gone (except for him, the Emperor), and a meritocracy was created (except for women). It is, after all, "Liberté, Egalité, and

Fraternité," not sorority, and only unmarried, son-less women whose patriarch had no other descendants, ascendants, or siblings could own or inherit property. The result: the oldest surviving son got it all, and Mom and the other children found themselves out on the streets.

It wasn't until 2001 that the law changed and the surviving spouse and *all* of the children (and the grandchildren of a predeceased child) were *prohibited* from being disinherited. Each was guaranteed something, but it's France, so it's complicated. There's a formula for distributing property, the exact percentage each person gets and the amount of tax s/he will have to pay to get it, depending on where they fall in a state-determined hierarchical relationship to the deceased—and there are now new unintended consequences, like having to wait five months to buy my house, and my neighbor's house being vacant and rotting for twenty-seven years, because now, instead of a single heir who can do any damned thing s/he wants, there are multiple heirs, *each* of whom can do any damned thing he or she wants—like *not* selling the property.

That's right. If one person—one of two, four, five, ten, or twelve—doesn't like the buyer's offer, or the buyer, buyer's clothes, spouse, accent, breath, or his/her own brother, sister, mother, aunt, uncle, niece, nephew, cousin, or cousin twice removed, s/he can refuse to sell, and there will be no sale, and the house will stay vacant for twenty-seven years, and if it's François's house it won't be two houses away where I can't see it, but right next door, where I can.

This is what I'm thinking as I sit on my terrace looking at the wooden fence and bushes where my thirty cypress trees once stood. The trees are long gone—ten cut so François and his garden could experience the sun, twenty downed in a storm—so they can't become an issue or cause trouble with a new neighbor, but my fence sags and my bushes are taller than the two-meter height law, and I often listen to music when I sit here, and when I entertain, I serve friends apéritifs here, and I know from my life and friends' stories that anything and nothing can cause trouble with neighbors, troubles I don't want or need in any country, but especially one where I can't speak the language and don't know my rights, which I suspect are zero. I've been lucky so far with Georges and Yvonne then François on one side, Bruno and Françoise on the other, and now two new neighbors behind me, whom I've finally accepted and gotten used to, mostly because I never see or hear them. For twenty-five years the only neighbors in the rear of the house were goats and sheep, and sometimes a horse. Then they were gone. Nothing changes in France for centuries, then everything changes—fast. . . . Like this:

I was looking through the living/dining room window at the built-by-hand, stone-by-stone, two-hundred-foot-long granite and slate wall behind my house, expecting to see a horse, sheep, or goats, grazing, bleating, baaing and whinnying, eating to their multiple stomachs' content. Instead, I saw the neighbor who lives up the hill, whom I've seen before, but never met, sitting on his tractor/lawnmower, getting ready to cut the grass. I prefer the sheep, horse, and goat mowing method to his loud, grumbly machine, but it's his land, and he does this periodically, so I'm not too surprised. I am surprised a few days later when I see a small cardboard *À VENDRE* sign staked in the lawn behind my house, making my third-worst French nightmare come true—nuclear accident (68 percent of French electrical power comes from nuclear energy); Le Pen victory (Marine Le Pen got 42 percent of the vote in the 2022 national election, 9 percent more than Hitler in 1933); new neighbors and houses in my backyard.

The next few weeks I spend a lot of time looking through the living/dining room window, missing what I haven't yet lost: the green hilly open space and view of the forest beyond—the reasons Donna said to paint the shutters green—and the horse, sheep, and goats being horse, sheep, and goats—not people . . . Definitely not people!

In my experience, French people can be very friendly, helpful, thoughtful, courteous, and kind, and thankfully almost everyone I've met has been. But French people can also be very assertive of their rights (which they know and I don't), and bigtime summer, weekend, National Fête Day, birthday, any day, *any* occasion *célébrants*, *fêters par excellence*, partying late into the night, playing loud (often terrible) music, and drinking to the dregs, not to mention having a bizarre proclivity for tiny, yappy—like recurrent beeping car horns—dogs, which is why I want to know exactly what that *À VENDRE* sign means: new neighbors in my neighbor's house high on the hill far away, or new neighbors, houses, roads, lights, sewers, and construction in my backyard? The thought of the latter makes me morose.

I return to California with lots of questions and no answers. Ella and Sharon keep me posted during the year as they did with the sewer work, only unlike the sewers, there is no work. Nothing is happening. Every so often, one or the other sends me photos of my house, the land behind it, and the *À VENDRE* sign to reassure me nothing has changed. And nothing does . . . until I receive a letter from *Géomètres Experts*, another enterprise I never heard of.

I look at the envelope, as I do with all mail from France, hoping it's junk, fearing it's not, and worried I won't know the difference. I open it and immediately recognize one key word—*cadastre*. It's one of those words whose meaning is the same in English and French . . . "A technical term for a set of records showing the extent, value, and ownership of land . . . ." ! Merde!

I Google Translate the letter expecting the worst, and sure enough, it's a cadastrophe! The letter is asking for permission to enter my yard to allow the measurement—the *bornage*—of the man on the hill's property lines. My first reaction is "Non," thinking maybe I can forestall the sale, but when I ask Sharon and Ella, Madame P, and Bruno and Françoise about the letter, they all say it's normal—*c'est normal*—and *Géomètres Experts* can go on my land whether I say yes or no. Besides, Bruno adds, "All the other neighbors, including us, have said yes," so I sign the letter, saying "Oui," hoping my cooperation results in my land being larger, the man on the hill's smaller, and the smidgen that's left won't sell.

Six months later, I pull into the driveway and see the tiny cardboard *À VENDRE* sign has morphed into a two-foot-by-six-foot banner, and as much as I dislike seeing it, I like seeing it, because as long as it's there, no one has bought the land and no one is building, though there are now lots of colorful marker flags planted in the ground like a crime scene, which to me it is: theft of my peace, quiet, privacy, and view.

I ask everyone I know what the flags mean and what they know about the sale of the house and the land and no one knows anything, but everyone has an opinion, and they all agree: the land will not be sold. Monsieur Charles, Ella, and Rick say it's too hilly and will cost too much to excavate. Sharon says it's too far from the main road and main sewer line and not worth the cost of connecting. Bruno and Françoise say the price of running water and electric lines, putting in streetlights, and adding an access road doesn't make sense when someone can buy a house that's already built and connected. Madame P just says, "Trop cher," too expensive.

I figure they live here, they're French (except maybe Sharon, Ella, and Rick); they know what people will buy and what they won't, so I sort of relax. But I'm an American—a male with a type A personality even if I now function at B–, and doing nothing is not an option. I wait a few days and formulate a plan. I've been to the ground floor of the *Mairie* many times to buy stamps, never to the first/second floor where the mayor's office is, but if not now, when? If not him, who? I call Madame P.

"Bonjour, Yvonne, c'est Mark"—as if she didn't know—"c'est possible vous demande a Marie-Luce"—her dear friend and neighbor who works at the *Mairie*—"fait le rendezvous avec le *Maire* pour moi, parce-que j'ai beaucoup les questions sur la terre à vendre a cote chez moi." It is possible you ask Marie-Luce make a meeting with the mayor for me because I have lots of questions on the land for sale beside my house?

She calls the next day and confirms "un rendez-vous" with the *Maire* the following week.

I arrive early, as I always do to important meetings, and say "Bonjour" to Marie-Luce, who directs me to a small, dark conference room to wait. I turn on the overhead light, and it's less dark. For some reason, this makes me happy, like they're being frugal with my tax money, not profligate. It makes me not want to waste their time or distract them from more important things, like adding a new speed bump or roundabout (which they don't), or allowing a baguette vending machine on city land (which they do). It's in this spirit that I greet the mayor, his assistant, and Marie-Luce when they enter the room. I stand, say "Bonjour," shake hands with everyone, comment on the weather—"C'est beau"—thank them for the meeting, and cut to the chase.

"A quelle a vendre?" I ask the mayor. What to sell? "Combien maisons?" How many houses? "A quelle taille?" At what size? "Ou est le lumieres public?" Where is the public lights? "Ou est le rue a la nouveau maisons?" Where is the street with the new houses? "Combien metres a cote chez moi?" How many meters beside my house? "Le egout ou fosse septic?" The sewer or septic tank?

The mayor doesn't know, or he's not telling. The only thing I find out is my neighbor's house on the hill and two lots behind mine are being sold individually. As best I can determine, everything else—streetlights, sewer, access road, size and location of house—is none of my business, up to the buyer, or both—*and* nothing can happen until I sign and approve the measurement—*le bornage*—the cadaster, which the mayor reminds me to do as I leave. "Signer *le cadastre*, s'il vous plaît."

"Oui," I say. "Bientôt." Soon. "Je pense." I think.

A few days later I go to *Géomètres Experts,* an office I've passed dozens of times, never looking through the window or wondering who they are or what they do. I knock on the door, and a preppily dressed, cheery young man greets me with a firm handshake and "Bonjour."

"Bonjour," I say, shaking his hand and wishing I wasn't wearing shorts and flip-flops. "Je suis Monsieur Greenseed. J'habite en Plobien. Vous-avez ecrie moi en le Étas Unis pour entre mon terre pour fait le *cadastre*." I am Monsieur Greenseed. I live in Plobien. You wrote to me in the United States to enter my land to make the land register

"Ah oui," he says, and goes to his files and returns with the forms I'm supposed to sign and a pen, neither of which I touch.

"C'est possible je regarde le carte?" It is possible I look at the map?

"Oui, bien sûr," he says, which, given the mayor's lack of information, amazes me, but not half as much as what he shows me on the color-coded map. The three-foot-high, two-hundred-foot-long granite and slate wall that I love to look at and years ago spent $1,000 to repair is not mine, but my neighbor's, the man on the hill, and will belong to whomever buys the land. The property dividing line is still the wall, but now the line is on my side of the wall, not his. For a moment, I'm pleased when I understand what he's saying: I'm no longer responsible for future repairs, which I know are needed and coming, or for retaining the hill. Then I'm worried: I'm no longer responsible for maintaining the wall or retaining the hill, and if my new neighbors aren't responsible, or don't care, or worse, decide to be done with it once and for all and cover the beautiful granite and slate with concrete—turning it into a freeway barrier—there won't be much I can do.

I ask Monsieur the same questions I asked the mayor, and, like the mayor, he doesn't know, or he's not telling. He hands me the forms and the pen. I point to my head, and say, "Je pense."

In the U.S., I get so much information—accurate, inaccurate, misleading, and false—that little is clear, and it's impossible to make important decisions, like whether or not to take a baby aspirin with confidence. In France, it's the reverse: there's not enough information. When I wrote my first book about living in France, I listed the actual price of the house I bought, and was told I couldn't, because in France that's private information, and to reveal it is against the law. In France, making private information public is a major no-no. The good news is these very strong privacy rights put huge limits and liabilities on Google, Facebook, and X. The bad news is they put the same limits and liabilities on me, which means it's impossible to make important decisions, like signing or not signing the cadaster with confidence. It's clear, the only way I'm going to get the information I want is to go to the source. I'm going to have to speak with my neighbor, the man on the hill—but not alone.

I know French people don't want to get involved in interpersonal matters, especially someone else's interpersonal matters, especially, *especially* a foreigner's, where they might have to take sides against their neighbor, a French person. Still, I ask Bruno—who knows the man on the hill—to set up a meeting, which is the easy part, and to come with me to translate, which is the hard part, and Bruno being Bruno, a kind, thoughtful, helpful, professional caretaker, agrees.

We arrive at the house after lunch and before *le goûter*, snack time—a time for business, not friends. Bruno introduces me and we shake hands. Monsieur is long and thin like a *haricot vert*, smiling, and seems friendly. Madame is pretty, petite, and like a compressed spring. I'm expecting more "it's-private-none-of-your-business" resistance, but when Monsieur directs us to their terrace, I see the table is set with plates, cutlery, napkins, glasses, and nibbles.

Monsieur, Bruno, and I sit, and Madame goes into the house. Bruno chats with Monsieur, and I look down the hill, marveling at their view of their land and trees, my house, the boats on the river/canal, the new (now twenty-year-old) lock, the hills and forest on the other side of the river/canal. I could sit here forever, but everyone else apparently has a life and things to do, so after Madame brings out wine, cider, iced tea, orange juice, and water (flat and sparkling), and we fill our plates with fresh fruit and nibbles, Bruno begins.

"Marc a beaucoup de questions," and he looks at me.

"Oui," I say, and I ask.

Madame explains to Bruno, who explains to me that the land is hers, inherited from her father (no thanks to Napoleon), and that Monsieur built this house on the hill. They're selling the land and the house—separately—because it's too much to maintain the way they want to maintain it—and I can see from the meticulousness and precision of their flower garden, fruit trees, veggie garden, and house how much work it is, and how much they have loved and maintained it, and now instead of being upset with them for selling the land behind my house, I feel sorry that they have to leave—and that I didn't meet them sooner.

Monsieur tells Bruno they are selling two lots plus their house, and he shows me where the new houses will be on the same color-coded map Monsieur Cadastre had. One is behind Bruno's house, which doesn't seem to bother him, and one behind my terrace, which does bother me, though I hope I manage not to convey it. The access road will be on the top of the hill near the forest, not on the bottom near my house. He doesn't know what size house will be built there: it's up to the new owners and the *Mairie*, which means I won't know until they're there. I don't ask about the septic tank or sewer line, but the new neighbors live above me, on a hill, and I know about gravity and water seeking its source, and know it can't be good.

We finish our drinks and shake hands all around. I thank them for being so forthcoming, though I don't know the word for forthcoming. "Merci, merci beaucoup pour tout les informations et les boissons," and I add, "Je voudrais ensign le bornage demain." Thanks for the information and drinks. I would like to sign the *bornage* tomorrow. On our way out, I mention, "Les pierre mur derriere mon petit bâtiment est tres fragile, je pense c'est tombe à bientôt." The stone wall behind my shed is very fragile, I think it fall soon.

The next day I initial the *bornage* and sign the *cadastre*.

Two weeks later, there's a knock on the door. I open it and see Madame. She explains by walking around the house, toward the shed, that she wants to examine the wall. I'm a little annoyed, wondering if she thinks I was lying to her. She looks at the wall, pushes a few of the larger stones, and sees they are loose. "Bon," she says.

Bon what? The stones are loose? I told the truth? What?

"Monsieur viendra le réparer." Monsieur will come and fix it. And he does, and it looks as good as the section of wall I paid $1,000 to repair years ago. I wish I'd known he owned it sooner.

Two years later the land sold, and now I have new neighbors, and I've been very lucky: no streetlights, no noise, no yappy dogs, no loud music, late parties, or septic-sewer leakage. All of which I'm grateful for and happy about, and is why I'm concerned about what happens to François's house—because the number of possible complications are infinite.

The village could allow a Maison des Jeunes et de la Culture that's open from seven in the morning to seven at night five days a week and every school holiday for kids three to fifteen to, among other things, learn how to play drums and flutes and appreciate blasting, brain-freezing music; a *moto club* for motorcycle enthusiasts; a *toilettage pour chien*, which is not a doggie dumping ground as I thought when I first saw the sign, but a place where yelping dogs get their hair, nails, teeth, ears—who knows what else?—cleaned, cut, polished, and wiped. . . . And I'm sure there are worse possibilities I can't even imagine.

As usual, what happens to me in France (and more and more in the U.S., too) is out of my control. I'll have to wait and see what happens—but hopefully not twenty-seven years . . .

My Sèche-Linge Is Dead, Long Live My Sèche-Linge

The weather's been balmy for weeks: seventy degrees and sunny; shimmering light; cloudless, International Klein Blue skies; starry, starry nights; the laundry flapping in the breeze, waving bonjour and au revoir to us when we arrive and leave, then the rain comes. It rains every day for three weeks, which is not atypical, but is bad timing, as we've had several dinners at the house, each using a table-for-eight tablecloth, multiple cloth napkins, and lots of dish towels. We also had friends visiting, adding sheets, bedding, and towels to Donna's normal, regular double and triple clothes changes per day and my well-planned ten-day recycling of everything I have to wear. During the third load on a wet and miserable day, the dryer stops. Dead, at 5:45 on a Saturday night, five days before we're leaving to visit the medieval walled citadel at Saint-Malo, eat Belon oysters in Cancale, and spend two nights on Mont Saint-Michel. Normally, I'd call Jean, but the last time I called him, he fixed it and said, "It's old. It's crap. Next time, you'll have to get a new one."

The good news is Donna and I recently bought a new one in California so we know what we're looking for: something simple, mechanical, not digital; no computers, LED screen, or impossible for stubby fingers to accurately touch touchscreen; a stainless steel drum, not plastic; clear, easy to read and operate setting knobs; large capacity; quiet; eco-friendly; front-loading; painless access to filters; long warranty; instruction booklet in English, and not made in China (not trustworthy) or France (looks great, doesn't work). In the U.S., we bought a made-in-America Speed Queen, the exact machine that exists in every Laundromat I've ever been in, only better, because I don't need tokens or a zillion quarters to run it.

DARTY, the store where I buy most of my household appliances, is a thirty-minute drive and closes at seven. I know this from years of many just-missed DARTY shopping experiences. I also know the store is closed Sunday, and if I wait until Monday the dryer will be delivered while we're in Saint-Malo.

We get in the car, and I drive like a Frenchman, taking the highway instead of the usual scenic route, avoiding all but four roundabouts, and arrive at the store at 6:10. By 6:20 we ascertain there are no Speed Queen or Speed Queen types, and every machine has computers and touch screens. We settle on an Electrolux because I think it's English and will have an information booklet in English, but even when I find out it's Swedish, built in Poland and Ukraine, and the information booklet is in every European language except English, I'm not dissuaded: it has only one dial that points to words, many of which I know, two buttons, and a tiny, toy touch screen.

We buy it at 6:55 on Saturday and schedule it to be delivered the following Wednesday, two days before we leave.

Wednesday afternoon, two youths arrive and quickly remove the old machine, set up the new Electrolux, and explain how it works—in French. There's an on/off power button, button #1: *marche/arrêt*, which is easy enough and clear. There's the dial, where the words I don't understand, like *rafraîcher* and *facile á repasser* (little ironing, easy ironing) now seem to outnumber those I do. Button #2, *séchage* (drying), sets the temperature and drying levels, which as far as I understand are very dry, dry, semi-dry, damp, and why bother? Pushing this button also sets the time of the cycle, like when, for instance, the dial is turned to *sport*, whatever that is, the *séchage* automatically sets (and cannot be changed) to the driest dry—very dry, which the machine, unbelievably, says takes ninety minutes to complete. To start the dryer, I have to touch something that looks like this >II on the tiny toy touch screen.

I thank the youths, walk them back to their truck, and wave goodbye as they drive away, then, to check my understanding, memory, *and* the Electrolux, I put a load of wash into the dryer, push button #1, *marche*, and turn the dial to *chemise*, shirts. The load is mostly socks, shorts, pants, and underwear—no shirts—but no other word seems close, and what the hell does the machine know anyhow? This isn't AI, it's a clothes dryer. I push button #2, setting it to dry in seventy minutes, and push >II. Nothing happens. I push >II again and again, turn the dial to *duvet* (there's no duvet in the load, either) and semi-dry in sixty minutes. I push *marche/arrêt* twice, and >II three times. More nothing. Now, I'm wondering if the machine is smarter than I think—or I'm dumber. I call Donna, show her everything I did and hand her the information booklet—hoping she can figure it out from the illustrations or the French—and return to the house. Thirty minutes later she comes back and says, "I can't do it."

Clearly, *hopefully*, this requires a French woman—and lucky for us we have one. Françoise and Bruno are next door, and they have a dryer, and they can read French—and there's nothing I've seen that Françoise can't do, except, apparently, this. After playing with the machine, reading the directions, pushing and turning and tapping and touching, she gives up and calls Bruno, who comes over and turns the dial, pushes the buttons, and touches the screen in a way I hope someone—like Donna—can duplicate.

She does, and we now have a Swedish-Polish-Ukrainian machine that cost more than the Speed Queen, dries less, takes longer, and has a hidden second filter that's impossible to see, get to, or clean. But it works, and we leave for Saint Malo two days later with clean, dry, and, in Donna's case, *facile á repasser*, easily ironed clothes in what feels like a minor but significant victory for the home team.

We return ten days later with suitcases filled with dirty clothes, an invitation to dinner at Yvonne's, and nothing to wear. Donna sorts a load of clothes and puts it in the washer. Ninety minutes later, I put the load in the dryer, push all the buttons, and get the same result I got last time—so I do what I did last time. I call, "Donna," and to my relief (and consternation), *she* remembers how it works, and it does.

Donna often says, "I'm the luckiest girl," and I hope she is, and continues to think so and say it, because *I* know *I'm* the luckiest guy—I'm in Plobien, going to dinner at my first friend's and guardian angel's home with the woman I married and love—and I have clean, dry, *rafraîcher* clothes to boot. Amen and Halleluiah! And when it's time to find, clean, or replace the second filter, it's comforting (and consoling) to know Donna can do it if/when I can't.

Shifting

Donna wants to learn how to drive a manual transmission car. I want her to learn, too—just not on my car. Years ago, I tried to teach her on my vintage forty-year-old Volvo P-1800—The Saint's car (just saying . . .). I love Donna, and I love my car, so when she asked for the fifth time, "Will you teach me to drive a stick?" I relented. Whatever wreckage she could do to the car was nothing compared to the damage I could do to us, which is why on a clear, sunny, 7:00 a.m. Sunday morning I drove us to the largest Safeway supermarket parking lot where the only possible things to hit were corralled shopping carts and scavenging pigeons. I parked at the farthest point on the hypotenuse from anything hittable except the pigeons, who didn't flap their wings, look up, move aside, stop eating, or give a damn.

"What do you think?" I say.

"It's too small."

I look at her and don't say what *I'm* thinking. That much I've learned over the years, though the parking lot looks to me as long, wide, and empty as Yankee Stadium on a non-game day.

"Let's try," I say with an enthusiasm I don't really have. "Watch what I do."

I depress the clutch pedal with my left foot and easily, smoothly, quietly shift into gear. "First is slightly to the left and up. All the way left and up is reverse. Be careful." Donna looks at me like, "I don't want to be here." I understand. I don't want to be here, either, but here we are—and I don't have the nerve to leave. I raise my left foot slowly and the car moves forward. "You just have to find where the gears connect—the point of engagement—and give it a little gas. Like this . . ." and I raise and lower my foot repeatedly—like, look hon, no hands—engaging and disengaging the clutch, moving forward and stopping, forward and stopping, forward and stopping. "See," I say, "it's easy."

I've been a teacher—a professional helper—all my adult life. I've taught thousands of students well and successfully for forty years, but teaching students about U.S. history and government, literature, and writing is not the same as teaching your wife to drive. For one thing, my students—at least as far as I know—didn't resent learning from me. For another, I didn't have to go home with them when they failed. There's a reason smart doctors don't treat family members, good lawyers don't defend family members, and I took driver's ed from Mr. F and not my dad.

I set the emergency brake, get out of the car, and walk behind it to the passenger side. Donna slides across the seat and over the gearshift, something I would never do with the engine running, and sits behind the wheel. I get in and close the door. Donna buckles up. There are no cars in sight, and we aren't going anywhere, but okay, I figure, it's good practice. Then she signals. Who? The pigeons?

I release the emergency brake and say, "Push the clutch pedal down—all the way to the floor."

She stretches, pushes, and moans, "It's too hard."

It *is* hard—it's a forty-year-old Volvo. "You can do it," I tell her.

She leans into the steering wheel, stretches her leg, reaches, pushes, and does it, like a new yoga position she's trying to master and hasn't.

"Great. Now, hold it there and shift."

She looks at me like the book says, like I'm from Mars. "Okay. I'll shift, you keep the pedal down."

I shift into first and my hand vibrates (not a good feeling), gears grind (not a good sound), and the car cries in agony, "You're killing me!" Somewhere, sometime soon I know I'll pay for this. . . . The car bucks to a stop. . . . For the next seventy minutes Donna pushes the pedal to the floor and slowly, slowly, slowly—slower each time—lifts her foot and searches for the engagement point while I offer encouragement: "Yes . . . yes, yes . . . THERE!" sounding like I'm in a porn movie . . . "Gas, gas, gas" . . . then, like a Pepto Bismol ad . . . Yelling "YESSSSS!" when she finds the point and moves the car a few inches, and "Ohhhhhhhhh" when we jerk and buck to a stop and the engine dies. After a dozen tries, I feel like I'm riding the bull at Gilley's. After two dozen, I *wish* I was riding the bull at Gilley's. I'm having visions of dropping the transmission right there, in the parking lot. All totaled, we travel about fifty feet, forty feet less than the distance from home to first—a gear we never got out of. The best news is no pigeons (or shopping carts) were harmed—or even disturbed—during this performance.

We do this three Sundays in a row and stop, each of us deciding sleep is a more productive use of our time. And that's that—until the January after my seventy-fourth birthday and I'm about to call Rob to lease a car for the summer in France, when Donna says, "You should think about getting a car with an automatic transmission in case something happens."

I don't ask what could happen, because I know—my father died from a massive heart attack. I also know she's right—I *should* lease a car with an automatic transmission, for her sake as well as mine, except I don't want to. I don't want to acknowledge the possibility and bring it closer, and I don't want to drive an automatic transmission, which is like a virtual visit to Paris instead of a real one, swallowing a pill instead of a *mousse au chocolat* for dessert.

I'm like all the men in my family—I like cars, and I like to drive fast. My mother's brother, my Uncle Henry, drove until he died at age ninety-eight. He lived in Queens and drove to Manhattan, something I stopped doing at fifty. He bought all of his cars at police auctions, mostly supercharged Dodges and Chevies. Every year, he got shorter—and he wasn't that tall to start with—and bought longer and more powerful cars. Around age ninety, no one—not even his sister, my mother—would ride in the car with him, but that only freed him to go faster, and he did. When Florida made it expensive and difficult to rent cars to people over eighty-five, he drove to Virginia, put his car on a car train, and picked it up in Miami. Then there was my Uncle Augie, who by the end was practically blind, which didn't stop him from driving his big white Cadillac Seville, often the wrong way down one-way streets, beeping his horn and screaming at the bastards to get out of his way. My father was a mini collector of sporty cars—and so is my brother: '56 Studebaker Power Hawk; '70 Corvette Stingray; '59 Mercedes 190 SL; '57 Thunderbird; '64 Avanti; '70 280Z; '69 Camaro;

'89 Grand Prix, and the crème de la crème, the car my mother used to go grocery shopping, a '68 Shelby 500KR convertible with 428 horsepower. Driving is in my DNA—and driving means a manual transmission . . . .

Still, I don't want to leave Donna (and probably me) in the lurch—on the side of the road, in the middle of the night, five minutes from a hospital, and unable to get there or call for help, because cell phone connections are often spotty on the coast, where we often are. So I do as Donna asks: I think about leasing a car with an automatic transmission, then I call Rob, lease a stick, and email Sharon.

"Do you know a good *auto école* in Loscoat with a woman instructor who speaks English?" Donna's French is good, but for important things, like life and death, her English is better.

Sharon emails back a few days later. "I found one. Her daughter says her mother is the only instructor in the area who speaks English."

Sharon sends me the brochure, and I send a check for a package of six lessons. Then, in May, I give Donna the brochure with a red circle around the six-lesson package, and say, "Happy birthday." She's amazed—surprised and happy I kept this on my radar and remembered. I'm happy, too, pleased that I addressed Donna's (and my) concerns without wrecking my car or our marriage—or leasing a car with an automatic transmission.

Eight weeks later we're in Plobien, and Donna calls to schedule her first lesson. She gets off the phone with a smile. It's the same smile she has when the Giants come from behind and win.

"So?" I say.

"I have an appointment in four weeks. It's the first time her Mom—Marie—is available."

Four weeks! It seems like an inordinate amount of time to wait, especially since I paid for the lessons two months ago. I figure Marie is either very successful and there's a long line of people who want to learn from her, or she's a failure and no one learns anything and everyone has to repeat. If I hadn't paid for the lessons and Marie wasn't the only English-speaking instructor in town and Donna wasn't so happy, I'd look for someone else.

"Do you want *me* to take you out?" I ask a few days later, making a half-hearted offer to teach her on the leased Renault that comes with 100 percent zero-deductible no-need-to-worry insurance.

"Not today," she says. "Maybe some other time."

I'm relieved. The only thing we regularly argue about is driving. Once, when I told her she was driving too slowly, she stopped the car and left me on the side of the road, making me walk home, which was even slower. I always think about that before I say anything about her driving, and half the time I decide to keep quiet. The other half, I don't. Won't. Can't—even though she has no tickets, points, or accidents on her record, and I have all three . . . .

Driving day finally arrives, and we both wake excited, probably for the same reason: I'm not the teacher. I am worried, though. I've driven past the *auto école* office numerous times, on different days at different hours, and the shades are always drawn and the door is shut. I'm also concerned about the rendezvous point, which isn't the *auto école* office. It's on the corner of a bend in the road *near* the office, on a very busy street that sharply C curves up a hill—a strange choice for a driving school with a brochure that stresses safety.

We arrive early, always a mistake in France, as no one is there. Ordinarily, I'd park and wait, but not on this street. I leave Donna on the corner, wave, call "Bonne chance," and get out of there before I have to fill out the official French accident form a fourth time. As it is, I'm convinced one of these years someone will read my driving record and refuse to lease me a car. Then Donna will drive, and I'll have to lease a car with an automatic transmission, and the need for these lessons will be naught.

Ninety minutes later I return, and Donna's standing on the corner where I left her. She gets into the car with her full-face smile, her happiest.

"So how did it go?"

"She doesn't speak English. Hello. Goodbye. Stop. Go. Yes. No. That's it."

"This is what we waited four weeks for?"

"She was good. It was hilarious. I had a great time. I like her. We laughed a lot."

I could have gotten the same result watching a Marx Brothers movie, but I don't say that. Nor do I ask, "Did you learn anything?" but two lessons later I find out. Donna can move the car, sort of—in first gear. Occasionally, she gets it into second. I know this because after the third lesson, she says, "Marie says I should practice with you. Will you take me?"

This is good news and bad. The good news is she trusts me. That's also the bad news. Failure is not an option. On Sunday afternoon, when the Intermarché is closed, I drive us to the parking lot—which is twice the size of the Safeway parking lot—where the only possible things to hit are a longer line of corralled carts, and a greater number of couldn't-care-less scavenging pigeons and gulls. This time, though, I'm relaxed: first, because I'm in Plobien, where I'm always more relaxed, and where, Donna says, I'm nicer; second, because it's not my car. It's also a newer car than my Volvo, and the pedal is easier to depress. So between the non-English-speaking hilarious French instructor and me, Donna hiccups the car down a straight, empty path in first, and, if I do the shifting, in second—and I feel terrific about it because Donna says, "I do better with you than Marie."

That was three years ago. Every year since, when I call Rob, I ask him about a car with an automatic transmission and lease a stick because I'm not yet willing to relinquish control, and I don't want to think about "just in case" or "what if"—both of which I think are far off.

I can still see, hear, read, reason, and react, and if I'm not on the coast I can call lots of people for help. . . . That's my right brain speaking. My left brain says life is a crapshoot, I'm not Methusulian, and what I don't want to happen will. Left to right, back and forth, forth and back, like a boomerang. . . . This year, my seventy-eighth, I've decided to lease a car with an automatic transmission. I'm comfortable with the decision. It feels like sound judgment, good sense, the right and smart thing to do, and I do feel better and safer for doing it—and also irretrievable, irremediable loss.

Loss, though, is not defeat (I tell myself), and driving with an automatic transmission is still driving, like flying on autopilot is still flying.

I'll continue to drive to Leclerc to shop, visit Gilles and Tatjana in Brest, take the scenic route to Quimper, the heather-hilled coastline to Crozon, and the C and D roads in Mont d'Arrée. I'll drive north to the Rose Granit Coast and the Emerald Coast, see the wildflowers at Cap Fréhel, visit Dinan, Dinard, Saint-Malo, and eat oysters in Cancale, and when I no longer can, Donna will, and when she no longer can, someone else will, because the point of living is to live, and even with an automatic transmission car, I do it best, fullest, and happiest when I'm in Plobien—which is why closing the house and leaving Plobien is the saddest part of every year.

L'Année Prochaine en Bretagne

A week before returning to California, Donna and I begin cleaning house, washing and drying laundry, visiting friends, and waiting for the latest, newest, last-minute, upending kerfuffle. The surprise isn't that it's coming—it always does—the surprise is *when* in the last week it will occur, *what* it will be, and *how* we, usually meaning I, will respond.

Over the years, there have been many: a downed tree, tumbled stone wall, blocked *dégraisseur*, a broken front gate. The biggest was when the old furnace stopped working four days before we were leaving, leaving no hot water for cleaning the house or us. Monsieur C was on vacation. I know because he told me. He always tells me when he's leaving town, which is something I wish my doctor in California would do. Monsieur C also gives me his cell phone number in case of an emergency, something else I wish my doctor would do. Monsieur C tells me when he's leaving and when he'll return, but he doesn't tell me who to call if something goes wrong when he's gone.

It's August, and every plumber in the phone book is either on vacation or knows it's me calling and doesn't answer his phone. I ask Yvonne, and she doesn't know anyone who's available to fix it. Nor does Sharon, Rick, or Ella, so I call the only person I know who *might* know someone—the son of the oil guy, who now is the oil guy. It's Saturday afternoon, and to my amazement he's there *and* answers his phone.

"Bonjour, Eric?"

"Bonjour, Marc."

"J'ai une probleme avec le chauffage. C'est marche pas, et pas d'eau chaude." I have a problem with the heating. It is not work and no hot water." It's a sentence I'm getting used to saying.

He doesn't say anything, but I hear him talking with a woman who I guess is more interesting than I. "Eric?"

"Oui."

"Connez vous un person fait le reparation?" Know you a person make repair?" Another sentence I wish I didn't know.

"J'arrive."

Thirty minutes later a car stops in front of the house. This is odd. He always comes with his truck. I go to greet him and see a woman is driving, which is also odd. French men don't usually have women drive them to work. *They* like to drive, lead, direct, control. . . . He opens the door and steps out, and I see he's wearing regular clothes—Sunday-I'm-not-working-today-clothes (pressed shirt, pants, dress shoes, not his blue overalls and work boots) and sunglasses, as if (1) the sun was out, which it isn't, and (2) he was at Majorca, which he's not.

"Bonjour," I call, very happy to see him, and hold out my hand to shake.

"Bonjour," he says, not shaking my hand, which is the biggest oddity of all, as Eric is a handshaker par excellence. "C'est Laure, ma femme," he says.

I shake her hand and say, "C'est Donna. Ma femme," and Donna and Laure shake hands. The four of us stand there looking at each other, with three of us actually seeing.

It turns out Eric was at the optometrist's office waiting for his eyes to dilate when he answered his phone, which was probably the reason for the silence on my end and conversation on his—"I'm going!" "Are you nuts?"—a conversation I've had many times in my life. As in most cases, nuts wins, and here they are. I point Laure to the shed where the furnace is so she can lead Eric, who has already walked into the bushes twice. All I can think is this doesn't bode well for me, Donna, the shed, the neighbors, or neighborhood.

I stand in the doorway, on alert and ready to run, watching Eric braille-read the furnace. Donna is on the lawn talking with Laure—even farther away than I am. Meanwhile, Eric takes the burner apart like a blindfolded soldier disassembling and reassembling a M4 carbine. Twenty minutes later, the furnace works, and we go into the house to celebrate, schmooze, and give thanks with coffee, tea, and galettes. Then Laure leads Eric back to the car and home, and Donna and I resume cleaning house.

Over the years, we've developed a system. My job is to clean the attic bedroom (where Donna works and visitors sleep), my study (where I write), the second-floor bedroom (where Donna and I sleep), the first-floor TV room, and the dining/living room. Donna's job is the attic bathroom, second-floor bathroom and toilet room, and the kitchen—a division of labor we're both happy with, as I don't want her putting my things where I'll never find them, and she doesn't want me cleaning any bowl, pot, pan, oven, shower, sink, or toilet she'll use.

We start with the rooms we no longer need—the living/dining room and the attic. We don't need the living/dining room because the only meal we'll eat at home is breakfast, which—depending on the weather—we eat on the terrace or in the kitchen. The only entertaining we do is when Monsieur Charles stops by for a Heineken, there's an unexpected knock-knock on the front door, and giving special thanks (like for Eric and Laure) for saving us, which we also do in the kitchen or on the terrace. We don't need the attic because the last overnight visitors are gone.

We begin the day after George and Marion leave.

I wake first and put on yesterday's dirty shorts and T-shirt—why dirty clean clothes to clean?—make a pot of coffee, and wait for Donna. She comes downstairs thirty minutes later looking spotless *and* fresh. I don't know how she does it. Her dirty clothes look cleaner than my clean clothes. She makes a pot of tea, lets it steep, and goes to the shed to start the first load of laundry.

Laundry is the alpha and zeta, the sine qua non of the week. Laundry starts each day and ends each day, the first load before breakfast, the last off the line or out of the dryer before we go out to dinner. Laundry is its own unit and measurement of time: LT, Laundry Time, kiss two to three hours goodbye.

Each load takes forty-five to ninety minutes to wash and one to two hours to dry—depending on rain, sun, wind, electricity, washing machine, and dryer, none of which I understand or can control. It's Donna's job because she prefers the bright, colorful clothes she bought to the gray and pink they become when I wash them. My job is hanging and unhanging, something we both agree I do well, and something we both favor, as the sun (when it's there) dries faster, better, and cheaper than the new almost-thousand-dollar Electrolux.

While Donna sorts and loads, I set the terrace table for breakfast: a thermos of coffee for me, pot of tea for her, half a baguette, brioche, apricot tart, *pain au chocolat*—something bakeryish—with butter and Yvonne-made quince (from our tree) confiture . . .

We eat slowly, watching the sun rise over the river and viaduct, girding ourselves to storm the Bastille, until neither of us can eat any more. Then I clear the table and drag the vacuum up thirty stairs to the attic. Donna fills a plastic bucket with paper towels, rags, sponges, brushes, and tile, mirror, toilet, shower, and floor cleaning products, and follows me—and the end of summer begins.

I vacuum the throw rugs and 150-year-old oak floor, Lemon Pledge the desk and chairs, shelve the books (by author) and magazines (by date), and make the bed. Donna washes and sanitizes the bathroom sink, shower, shower curtain, toilet, and floor. It takes us all morning. When we're done, we seal the third floor like it's a crime scene with the unspoken understanding that short of an absolute, dire, unimaginable, can't-wait-any-longer diarrheic emergency, then and *only* then, after swearing and attesting to such and agreeing to clean it 1,000 percent better, can the seal be broken and the toilet be used, which thankfully has never happened.

I drag the vacuum down the thirty stairs, leave it in the dining room, the next room I'll clean, and unhang and hang a load of laundry. Donna leaves the bucket and cleaning supplies in the kitchen, where she'll spend the next six days cleaning one appliance or cabinet a day, and puts another load of laundry in the wash. Then we shower, dirtying two more towels, creating two more loads to wash, adding two LTs, and dress in clean clothes (which will also need to be washed), and go to Yvonne's for lunch. Everyone wants to see us before we leave, and everyone wants to see us last. It's France, so there's a hierarchy, and every year begins and ends with Yvonne.

"Bonjour, bonjour," Donna and I call as we enter the open front door and exchange cheek kisses with Yvonne, giving her four each, which hardly seem like enough. Donna hands her a bouquet of red roses and white lilies from our garden, and Yvonne adds them to the vase of purple and white hydrangeas on the counter. On the table, a half-inch-high plateau of crêpes is surrounded by a quarter kilo of butter, bowl of sugar, and Yvonne-made apricot, strawberry, and quince jams. . . . She's making my favorite dish—dessert.

"Asseyez-vous, asseyez-vous," she says, pulling a chair away from the table and handing me a bottle of unlabeled, friend-made cider that I know from experience has double the alcohol of the Kool-Aid they call *cidre* and sell in the store. I pop the cork and fill our glasses, though I know Yvonne won't drink. She never does. She won't eat, either, even though she's cooked a feast. She continues buttering the skillet, pouring and spreading more batter, making more crêpes, telling us to eat, eat—"Mangez, mangez" —which we ignore, saying, "Arrête, arrête, asseyez vous," Stop, stop, sit down, which she ignores until there are at least forty and she's satisfied there are enough. Then she sits.

"Santé," I say, holding up my glass of cider, and Donna and I drink. Yvonne doesn't. "Mangez," she says, and Donna takes a warm, moist, almost humid crêpe and places it on her plate, then I do, then Yvonne: Yvonne folds hers in half and picks at the crispy edges; Donna covers hers with strawberry jam and eats it like a pancake with a knife and fork; I lather mine with butter, cover it with apricot jam, fold it in quarters, and eat it with butter-dripping fingers like a slice of oily New York pizza.

As if on cue, Yvonne begins recounting her favorite Marc stories: when I asked for "*jus de vache*" (juice of cow) instead of milk, "*un poulet beaucoup de promenade*" (a chicken that walks a lot) for a free-range chicken, "*un kilometre sauccison*" instead of a kilogram, searching the market for "un bay leaf," *une feuille de laurier*, that she later showed me grows in my yard. . . . She cherishes the stories, and I cherish how she tells them, how she remembers them, and how much pleasure they bring her and Donna and me. I'm waiting for her to ask if I'm happy here. It's part of our routine—like "Who's on First." Asking is her way of validating all that has happened between us. Answering is my way of saying thanks.

"Es-tu heureux d'avoir acheter une maison ici?" Are you happy you bought a house here, she asks.

"Oui. Bien sûr. Merci à vous." Yes. Sure. Thanks to you. Meeting her, buying the house, and marrying Donna are three of the most implausible—and phenomenal—events in my life.

Two hours later, Donna and I clear the table and carry the dishes to the sink, but Yvonne won't let us wash them. We may be family, but we're also guests. We set a date for dinner the following week, right before we leave for California, because every year starts and ends with Yvonne. Then, with lots of "*À bientôts*" and "*À la prochaines*," she hands me a mound of crêpes wrapped in tinfoil and ushers us out of her house so she can clean her kitchen.

We drive back to our house, hang a load of laundry, take a long nap, unhang the laundry, and go to dinner at McDan's, a seasonal pop-up that's popped up and expanded every summer for the past thirty years. The first time I went there it was a single caravan selling roasted chicken, seemingly one thigh, wing, leg at a time. Now, it's three caravans: one is a full bar; one is for ice creams, sorbets, cotton candy, and sweets; and one is for serious eating—steaks, hamburgers, kebabs, chicken, and sometimes pizza. Donna and I always go there our last week to eat one more gyro sandwich, sit vigil at one more ocean sunset, and say goodbye to Monsieur Dan.

As usual, it's jammed. People of all shapes, sizes, ages, physical conditions, and attire—from near-naked to sweat-shirted and knee-length-sweatered—are eating, waiting to eat, and standing in line to order what they're going to eat. Monsieur Dan is behind the bar.

"Bonsoir," Donna and I say in unison and each shake his hand.

"Bonsoir," he says, and pours us each a glass of rosé. Donna prefers red; I prefer white, but who's complaining? This is a first.

"Merci, merci," we say, and he nods and walks away to serve someone else. I get in a line that really is a line to order two gyros and *frites* and another glass of wine each—a red and a white. Donna takes the glasses of rosé and settles at a table facing the mile-long beach and the sea. It takes a while for the food to arrive, but when it does, it's what we've been waiting for: hot, salty fries (not greasy) and gyro sandwiches that are a sriracha (me)/tzatziki (Donna) mess to eat. We finish at dusk—ten o'clock—as the sky streaks yellow, orange, pink, and rouge, and the sun slips into the ocean.

We go to the bar and say "Au revoir" and "A l'année prochaine" to Monsieur Dan, and he says, "Je pars en octobre pour une tournée de deux semaines dans l'ouest américain qui se termine à San Francisco. Serez-vous là alors?" which warms my heart. He's going to be a stranger in a strange land—on a tour of the western U.S., Los Angeles, Bryce, Zion, Las Vegas, Monument Valley, Grand Canyon, ending in San Francisco— and he wants to know he has a friend, and that someone—*us*— has left the light on for him.

Donna gives him our phone numbers, a two-cheek kiss, and says, "A bientôt á San Francisco . . ." and the first day of our last week ends.

The next morning Donna washes a load of laundry and cleans the stove. I clean the dining room and hang the load. We're having lunch with Monsieur Charles and dinner at our favorite pizza place in Loscoat with Françoise and Bruno.

At 11:30, I drive into Monsieur Charles's courtyard. Tom, his dog, is waiting to greet us, waving his tail and barking "hello." Monsieur Charles comes out of the barn, his smiling, happy-to-see-you cherubic face letting us know he's looking forward to a day of drink, food, and nonsensical French that only he and a few other highly skilled and immeasurably patient interpreters can translate from me, and real conversation from Donna.

We exchange "Bonjours," handshakes, and cheek kisses and follow him into his house—an old, stone farmhouse, like ours, but not like ours, because he *is* a farmer (hectares of corn), and we're not, and because we, as newcomers, prefer the original dark-beamed ceilings, wide-plank oak floors, fireplaces, retro tile, antique furniture, and quiet, and he, an original, prefers the new: bright tile, light wood, Scandinavian-style furniture, and a fifty-inch flat-screen TV that's on, showing up-to-the-second twenty-four-hour news.

We sit at the kitchen table and he rips open bags of chips and nuts to nibble and asks, "Une boisson?" A drink?

"Oui," I say. "Bien sûr." It's why we're here—for apéritif before lunch. Donna has *kir pêche* (peach). I have Ricard. Monsieur Charles has whiskey. It's 11:40. Our lunch reservation is at 1:00, and the restaurant is fifteen minutes away, which gives us an hour and five minutes to drink. Every year, I tell myself I'll nibble and drink less and eat more lunch, and every year I don't. This year is no different. By the time we leave for the restaurant, Donna and I are full and looped.

The restaurant is the same one my girlfriend and I ate in the first night we were in Plobien thirty years ago. There's a third owner now, but the menu hasn't changed, and I order what I ordered then—*Gambas Brochette*. Donna orders a *salade de gésier*, gizzard salad, the thought of which makes me gag. Monsieur Charles has an apéritif, steak, frites, *haricots verts*, *salade*, wine, ice cream, and coffee. During the meal, we talk about his new lot of fifty chicks (I don't ask about the old lot), the pig he's fattening for *saucisse* and *roti de porc*, the new lawn he's going to plant at our house, and his latest plan to do in the moles. At this point, I think they bother him more than me. To me, they're nature and almost neighbors; to him, a challenge to his excellence. . . . When we leave the restaurant I'm ready to sleep, and after I unhang and hang a load of wash, I do.

In the evening, Bruno, Françoise, Donna, and I go to the pizza place for dinner, because Donna and I insist. Bruno would rather cook, but going to the pizza place is part of our leaving routine. Aldo, the pizza guy, now knows what I want without my asking, which is a good thing, because the first dozen times I asked no one understood what I said: ancholade, anshowlade, anshwayade—*anchoillade*, anchovy and capers pizza.

We walk in and Aldo calls out "Anchoillade," and I nod. Marie, his wife, who's also the waitress, says "Bonjour" and sits us at one of the four tables. Donna orders a pizza with green salad on top, Françoise, a pizza with a sunny-side up egg on top, and Bruno with Brie on top of mozzarella, Emmentaler, and chèvre. . . . Thirty years, and I still can't believe what French people (and now Donna) put on pizza.

While we're eating, single guys, couples, and groups stop by to sit at the bar, chat, drink, and watch weird game shows and sexy music videos on the TV. Aldo welcomes and talks with them all. Marie and their two adult kids serve them all and clean up. Every now and then Aldo looks at me and nods. Marie watches to see if we need anything—napkins, hot sauce, water, wine—and twice tells us the pizza is good. "C'est bon," she says—a statement, not a question—and I say, "C'est meilleur." It's the best—and it is, with a crust that's thinner than Original Ray's in New York City.

"Au revoir," I say to Aldo when we leave. "Merci pour tout. Nous sommes parti a Californie cette semaine." Thanks for everything. We went to California this week. Then I shake his hand and two-cheek-kiss Marie. Donna does the same, and Bruno and Françoise watch, astonished. Who kisses their pizza maker's wife? We do.

And so it goes . . .

Every day we wake later and tireder, and in my case, dirtier. We launder, clean house, and say goodbye to friends, and since goodbyes in France are very important, and since everything important in France takes place around food, we eat—a lot! We have a series of Last Suppers (and Lunches). That's how I think of them, as communions, not our version of the film *La Grande Bouffe*.

We say goodbye and eat lunch with Ella and Rick; dinner with Hugo and Martine; dinner with Gilles, Tatjana, Ael, and Emil; lunch *and* dinner (because we're at their house all day) with Jean-Pierre, Joël, Gaël, Marie, David, and their kids; lunch, dinner, breakfast, and lunch with Bruno and Françoise because Bruno is on call, and we spend a night at their first house, two hours away, where their neighbors want to feed us as much as Bruno and Françoise do: we have apéro and nibbles at Jean-Claude's; more apéro, barbecue chicken, and drinks at Jocelyne and Pierrick's; apéro, cassoulet, drinks, and gateau with Michel and Yvette. I look and feel like a top when we leave. Donna's worried about lassitude, something she never worries about in the U.S. The penultimate evening we have our next-to-last Last Supper with Yvonne, her son and daughter-in-law, Henri and Renée, Monsieur Charles, and Yvonne's friends and neighbors Marie-Luce, Alain, and their daughter, Pauline. The first twenty-plus years we ate our very last Last Supper at Yvonne's house, but now, given the number of people, the amount she cooks, and her refusal to allow anyone to help her, Donna and I decline to eat there. Instead, we compromise and eat at a restaurant of her choice—always a crêperie—where the crêpes are never as good as hers, and sometime during the meal she looks at me, like "See . . ." and I look at her, like "I know, I know, I know . . ."

By the end of the week, only our bedroom and bathroom need cleaning. Laundry is down to one small load a day (which takes as long as a large load), and there's been no kerfuffle. I'm trying not to think it, but I'm thinking, Holy, holy cow! Maybe this is the year.

The last day begins—like a mantra or Lauds—with laundry. While the machine washes, I clean our bedroom, Donna cleans the bathroom and toilet, and the shower while she's showering. Then we dress, pack our suitcases, hang the last laundry, and drive to Loscoat to say goodbye to our village friends:

Au revoir to Eric and Manu, telling them everything still works, thanking them for another successful digital experience, and assuring them they're not legally responsible for anything I wrote;

Au revoir to Madame J and her son and grandson, thanking them for thirty years of selecting the best fruit and veggies for us to eat, *aujourd'hui* (today), *demain* (tomorrow), or *mardi prochain à quinze heures dix* (next Tuesday at 3:10 p.m.);

Au revoir, Yannick, whose wide-eyed fish chilling on ice are so fresh they look fake;

Au revoir, young couple and longtime woman assistant, whose names I don't know, third owners of the charcuterie where I reserve my *poulet libre*—free-range chicken—and buy homemade paté and non-boudin, non-andouille sausages;

Au revoir, Claude and Annie, who no longer wince— or even blink—when I open their door without an appointment and ask an insurance question I'm sure no one has asked before—at least not in the way I ask it;

Au revoir, Fred, at the *Maision de la Presse*, who hosted a book party for *I'll Never Be French* when it was published in French and served a punch so potent it got him, Muriel, Jean, and everyone who came into the shop bombed before 11:00 a.m.;

Au revoir, Michelle and Dominique: she English, he fourth-generation French baker, winner of the Best *Gâteau Breton* in Brittany award, caught in changing times. Neither of their two daughters wants to spend a lifetime waking up at four in the morning to make cakes and tarts for others. It's a widespread generational dilemma—and no one in Plobien can imagine life without their *patisserie.* Donna and I give Michelle four cheek kisses each and shake Dominique's hand, thanking them for thirty years of confectionary perfection, beginning with his dad—the third generation—making my birthday party cake and ending with us buying a strawberry tart for tonight and four croissants and apricot tarts for tomorrow.

We visit Monsieur Charles to say "Au revoir" and give him the five remaining Heinekens.

We bring Yvonne our leftover eggs, butter, yogurt, tomatoes, carrots, and peaches along with food and supplies from a huge shopping I do that I wish was large enough to last her until we return. I know she has Henri and friends and neighbors to help, but being able to partially return thirty years of her lifesaving interventions makes me feel better and eases my guilt for leaving, and not doing more. We exchange hugs, cheek kisses, and more hugs—there are never enough—and don't say *au revoir.* She stands in her doorway and waves as we leave, and Donna and I wave back, all of us calling, "Bisous, bisous, bisous," kisses, kisses, kisses . . .

Our very, very Last Supper is with Sharon and Jean . . . We bring them a bag of our exotic leftovers—balsamic vinegar, hot sauce, chutney, baked beans, and peanut butter (which is not easy to find in France)—and the strawberry tart we bought at the *pâtisserie* for dessert. We arrive on time—at six o'clock— because we have to leave at eleven, to wake at three, for the 6:15 morning flight to Paris and ten o'clock flight to San Francisco.

Donna pulls the rope and rings the bell to let them know we're here. I open the door using the secret way and carry the bag of groceries—grosseries?—up the stairs, and smell, then see, Sharon is making *filet mignon de porc* with tiny browned potatoes and green beans, all my favorites. She's set the table with her mother's Irish linen tablecloth, porcelain dishes, designer silverware, and crystal glasses that she only uses at special times with special people, like us tonight.

"Bonsoir," I say and give her four cheek kisses. Donna hugs her and gives her four more. Jean comes out of the bedroom and greets us with "Bonsoirs" and more cheek kisses and leads us to the living room for apéritifs.

He passes olives and radishes, slices sausage, and keeps our glasses full. Sharon joins us, and we talk about his book—*L'Oeuf Cosmique et la Soupe Primordiale* (*The Cosmic Egg and Primordial Soup*), a comparison of cultural (Aztec, Tibetan, Maori), scientific (quantum theory, relativity, big bang), and religious (Adam and Eve, the Four Creations, the Golden Chain, Pan Gu and Nü Wa) explanations of human origin. It was recently published in French, and he wants to translate it into English and wants Sharon, Donna, and me to help him—or says he does—even though he argues over every change and suggestion we make.

I understand—he's French; he wants rules and structure and certainty about commas, dashes, semicolons, and colons, and Sharon, Donna, and I don't agree. He hates it when we break his long, beautiful, circuitous French sentences into shorter declarative American English (Donna and me) or Canadian English (Sharon), and when we change words—like exposition and exhibition, whose meanings are reversed in English and French. But the worst of the worst for him are quotation marks, as French, British English, and American English use them differently. . . . We're talking about his book and differences in French and British English and American English writing, but I know, because Sharon told me, he's preoccupied with his upcoming doctor appointment.

Jean doesn't trust doctors, hospitals, or anything he didn't build or fix himself. When he lost his hearing in one ear, he built himself a hearing aid from an old transistor radio. But he knows his limits. When his heart valve began leaking, he had it replaced, although I'm pretty sure only after he tried to build his own. He chose a pig's valve as a replacement, and now, ten years later, he needs another, and he's contemplating another pig's—which has worked fine—or a human or mechanical one. I think he's leaning toward the mechanical just so he can see how it works. "Which do you think you'll choose?" I ask him.

"I don't want to talk about it," he says, but this is France, and he's French, so he does, and we do, along with his book and the stupidity and shortcomings of American and Canadian English.

At eleven o'clock, when our plates are clean, glasses empty, and the strawberry tart all gone, Sharon reminds us, "It's time to go," because neither Donna nor I want to leave them, their table, Plobien, or France. We exchange multiple cheek kisses and hugs. Then Donna and I get in the car, and we all wave goodbye until they and we are out of sight.

Ten minutes later, we're home. I unlock the front door—which opens smoothly and easily in the cool night air—and trundle up the stairs to shut the bedroom window *before* I turn on the lights, hoping to block hungry mosquitoes (there are amazingly few), buzzing flies, suicidal moths, and crazed or curious bats. We're the only Americans in the village, and the only people who sleep with the windows *and* shutters open so we can hear the river flowing and feel the cool, fresh night air on our skin, but it's France, and it's not as easy as that, because—I'll never know why—there are no screens.

I shut the window, turn on the lights, and we get ready for bed. Then, when Donna is under the covers and settled, I set the alarm for 3:00 - a.m., turn the last light off, open the window, hear the river, feel the breeze, and hope for the best: no mosquitoes, flies, moths, bats, or kerfuffle.

I lie there taking inventory: house clean; oil tank full; gas off; all windows and shutters, except our bedroom, closed and locked; refrigerator empty; garbage dumped; dehumidifier on; outdoor furniture in; plugs pulled; shed locked; furnace off; house stocked with paper towels and cleaning supplies for Ella; Rick has the list for this year's work. . . .

I wake before the alarm and begin the final steps of leaving, starting with shutting the bedroom shutters for the first time since the day I arrived. I open the window wide to grab the shutter, and Whooooooooosh—something huger than a moth and smaller than a Volkswagen flies into the room, screeching, *kerfuffle!* I shut the window and rush to close the door, hoping whatever it is is still in the room and not flying around the three-story house, freaking out, crapping on everything, or committing suicide.

I'm pretty sure it's a bat—there have been three in the house—and I'm thinking about what to do. If it is a bat I should open the window, hope it's not crazy or rabid or Dracula, and let it find its way out. If it's not a bat, opening the window could allow in more of whatever it is. I'm pondering what to do when Donna turns on the light, and I see, cringing on top of the armoire, a dove, probably one of the pair that roosts on the roof and greets us when we arrive and leave.

Instinctively, it moves to the far back corner of the six-foot-high armoire where neither Donna nor I can reach it. . . . I look at the clock . . . It's 3:10. We still have to shower, dress, load the luggage in the car, lock the house, and be on the road by 4:00 to get to the airport by 4:45 to return the car and check in by 5:00 for our 6:15 flight, and that bird isn't going anywhere.

The choice is to sneak out of the room, shut the door, and let the bird slowly die and rot (and smell), or miss the flight and pay Air France beaucoup dollars to change the tickets because I'm pretty sure this won't qualify as a refundable emergency. That's what *I'm* thinking, but Donna and the bird have better ideas. She opens the window and throws a pillow at the bird, and it flies out the window as moths and flies fly in (and, hopefully, painfully die). I shut the shutters and lock the window, then shower and dress in my travel outfit: old Giants sweatshirt and jeans that won't get ruined or look any the worse after twenty-plus hours of travel. Donna wipes the shower clean as she showers and dresses in a multicolored striped Breton shirt, as if she's going to dinner or a party, and we're ready—but not before completing our annual ritual.

We walk through the house, top down. "Bye room," we say to the attic, Mom's favorite room, where Donna sits, reads, works, and is warm. "Bye tiled bathroom" that Martin built, Rick retiled, where Jean fixed a leaking skylight in the middle of a stage three storm. Down fifteen stairs to my study. "Bye room" where I write every day, never knowing until months later if anything I wrote is any good. "Bye room" to Rick's newly built shower and marble-tile bathroom. "Bye room" to our bedroom with the oak armoire and desk I bought with my mom the first year I bought the house, and the Japanese banner, obuku, and brush drawing a Japanese artist made for Donna when we visited Sanary with Bruno and Fançoise in Provence. Down another fifteen still shiny, Hugo-finished stairs. "Bye stairs." To the TV room with the light-oak book-case I bought at an antique fair, and the new TV that replaces the old TV that Yvonne and her family, Monsieur Charles, and Breton friends gave me for my fiftieth birthday in the hope that I'd learn French—real French, not the pidgin patois I still speak. "Bye room." Up one step into the living/dining room that hooked me into buying the house, with its exposed granite walls, cathedral ceiling, two fireplaces, terra-cotta floor, and the pine country table for eight. "Bye room." Down a step and into the kitchen with its 130-year-old tile floor, beamed ceiling, Rick- and-Martin-made cabinets, "new" fridge and stove, and tiny sink and dishwasher. "Bye room."

I close and double-lock the front door I know I'll never replace. Donna goes to the car and waits as I walk through the moonlit yard. "Bye roses, hydrangeas, apples, quince, bay leaves, and trees. Bye, Yvonne's used-to-be garden, Monsieur Charles's lawn. Bye, bye, bye." The only thing I don't say good-bye to are the moles, because they're the one thing I'm certain aren't leaving.

I get in the car, my shoes wet from the morning dew, and drive past the new gate that, like the shutters and bedroom window, is always open while we're here. I get out of the car and close the gate and latch it shut. We sit there for a minute, taking it all in, the new gate, green shutters and door, the yard, Rick's new stone driveway, and the house—the gorgeous, beautiful, light and life-changing house. "Bye house," we say, and wave. "Bye house."

I wave goodbye to François and his house, wondering who and what will greet us next year. "Bye," I call out as we pass Bruno and Françoise's empty house, "Bye river, bye viaduct, boats, boat people, *pâtisserie*." I stop at Yvonne's and hang a plastic bag with two croissants and apricot tarts on her front door. "Bye, Yvonne . . ."

"L'année prochaine en Bretagne." Next year in Brittany, we sing as we drive out of town. Donna's voice is strong, her words clear, confident, and sure. Mine are a hope and a prayer . . .

Afterword

Back when I thought I was Methusulian, I didn't think very much about endings. Why should I? They were nine hundred years away. Now I'm seventy-eight, and I do.

I don't feel old, but I guess I am. I recently filled out a survey for a theater in San Francisco and checked the box indicating my demographic: 65 and over. It was the last box on the list, and it startled me. It still does: There ought to be a box for 75 and over, 80 and over, 90 and over, and 100. Clearly, this survey was written by a younger person, someone who doesn't yet know the differences between sixty-five, seventy-five, eighty, and ninety, who has never met my ninety-four-year-old Aunt Norma, or heard her say, "I wish I were eighty again."

I know what she means. I'm the same person I was when I bought the house in Plobien, and I'm not.

When I was younger, I thought I could transform the future—stop *and* speed up time—and change things that never seem to change, like human nature. I wanted to eliminate greed, selfishness, authoritarianism, class, abuse, racism, poverty, hunger, colonialism, imperialism, and oppression. I was all for the creation of the New Man, which at the time included the New Woman. I believed in Che and Mao and revolutionary change, but that was then, and this is now.

Now, I'm a preservationist and conservationist, *not* wanting to change the world, wanting instead to preserve and conserve what's good and right and beautiful (like my white shutters). Now, I know there's a time for everything—a time for revolution *and* for preservation—and that my time is speeding up as I'm slowing down.

I began planning my non-future when I turned seventy-five. Donna and I bought our own square meter of earth, large (or small) enough for two urns and two earners—not in the sun, it's too hot; not by the road, there's too much traffic, noise, and pollution; as near a tree and shade as possible; not near running water (I can't swim) and not in the flatlands, but on a hill with a view of the San Francisco Bay. Of course, this is nuts, but who cares?

More and more as I live and write, place is important to me. For living, as for dying, location, location, location matters. So do markers, identifiers, memorializers, acknowledgments, thanks, and remembrances—On this spot . . . In this building . . . At this corner . . . Born, Died, Lived, Wrote. . . . So now Donna and I have our one square meter of earth and stone s/he-was-here markers in perpetuity—or however long the cemetery keeps its license, pays its taxes, and doesn't get bought and condominiumized.

Donna, of course, doesn't worry about any of this. She's Buddhist and has a round-trip ticket. Mine, though, I suspect, is one-way. Donna was born and raised in Berkeley and has lived in the East Bay all her life. Ninety-nine percent of her large—sixty-three-member—family live there, too. I was born in Brooklyn, raised on Long Island, went to school for six years in Madison, Wisconsin, lived and taught in Greensboro, North Carolina, for two years, and dwelled at seven different residences in four different cities over fifty-plus years in California. The longest I've been at one address is my thirty years in Plobien . . .

New York, California, and Brittany. When I'm in California, people think I'm a New Yorker. When I'm in New York, they think I'm Californian. When I'm in Brittany, they think I'm English. In America, people of color think I'm white, and white people think I'm Jewish, which (depending on which white people) may or may not make me white. . . . I think I'm a New York-California-Breton-Jewish-democratic-socialist, and since location is important to me, I want to reside in three places: my square meter in California with Donna and her family, in New York with my family and Donna if she wants to mix with us, and Plobien with Donna if she wants to join me.

This is how the book originally ended, but it's not where the story ends.

My friend Fred, who years ago visited me in Plobien with his wife Ann, recently asked, "How did you ever succeed in France?" and stumped me. It's a question I've never asked myself because I've never thought of my life in France as a success. I look at myself and see shortcomings. In a land where words and language are foreplay, I can't play: I can't read my mail, understand TV game shows, or join regular, normal conversations with French people; I need help, explanations, and interventions to use the phone and operate my clothes dryer.

My deficiencies and flaws are what I see and have written about, but now, thanks to Fred and lots of emails and conversations with strangers, I also see what people who are not me see:

accomplishment, a full life, a good life, maybe even *the* good life. I live a good life in California and the U.S., but according to people who know me, I live a better/healthier life in France. Donna happily says it's because in France I'm more like her: more accepting, letting go, feeling and expressing gratitude. In the U.S., she unhappily says she's becoming more like me: pushy, argumentative, and worried—and therein we two do meet.

I'm now like on page 175 of a 200-page book. I have a sense of an ending that I didn't have on page 3. In the beginning, I know the story will end (I can see the last page) but I'm not thinking about it—just like when I bought the house. At forty-seven, I looked at older people and didn't see myself. At seventy-eight, I look at younger people and think, "You have no idea."

I remember when my grandparents were my age now. All they seemed to talk about was what was and what used to be. They'd pass a building, house, park, theater, store, and say, "Remember when . . .?" or "There used to be . . ." and now I'm doing it, too. To my amazement and chagrin, I've become a "used to be," "remember when" kind of guy. My world is a palimpsest: I see what is and what was, what's there and what's not . . . I'm a time traveler with double vision. . . . When I first came to Plobien, I saw what was here and I was astonished. Now, I see what's gone, and I'm even more so . . .

I drive home from Sharon and Jean's, alert to stop for bunnies that no longer hop across the road. I open the shed door and look for the fox Yvonne told me she once found sleeping there, and for the tiny frogs that used to make their way, like a pilgrimage, from the river to my clothes dryer. I sit on the quay and see fisher-men-women-and-kids who no longer cast from the quay or boats, fishing for salmon that are no longer there. I walk through the park across the street where there used to be trees, campers, Boy Scouts, Girl Scouts, and Roma, and see sheep grazing, frolicking, fattening, well on their way to becoming *gigot d'agneau* (leg of lamb) and chops. I remember the swan family, heron, egret, and fireflies, the donkey who lived down the road, and the sheep, goats, and horse grazing behind my house. Now, the only animals I regularly find are moles plowing my yard, doves roosting on my roof, bees in my chimney, bats, and flies.

I miss the huge veggie garden Yvonne had at my house, filling half my yard, and her almost-daily visits to tend it; the village nautical fête with the best fireworks I ever saw; the market that used to be on both sides of the river now squeezed into a parking lot next to the *poste*; my thirty cypress trees. . . . Three charcuteries are down to one, four boulangeries down to two, one of which is a drive-through with a red vending machine that sells fourteen different kinds of three-minute pizzas 24/7 in the parking lot. The bike store where I had my bike serviced is gone, and so are four hotels and their restaurants. The bars survive, and the banks, the coiffeurs, crêperies, churches, *supermarchés*, eyeglass stores, pharmacies, movie theater, and old guys (who are mostly younger than I) playing boule alongside the quay.

There's a new Olympic-size indoor swimming pool, new residence for seniors, new medical clinic, firehouse, homes, and businesses—a chandlery, 5G tower, real estate offices, wine shop—and the occasional traffic jam on the bridge carrying people to and from the coast and piggies and chickies to market. Sailboats, motorboats, catamarans, and restored old fishing ships pass through the lock on their way to the ocean, or to moor on the quays in Plobien and Loscoat—and the light, the brilliant North Sea, Gauguin, Monet, Matisse light I fell in love with the first day I was in Brittany remains, as do the bigger than Big Sky skies, dandelion-clock clouds, red, white, and blue bowling-ball-size hydrangeas, shamrock-green forests, Riviera-like beaches, forty-foot tides, rugged craggy coasts, granite viaducts, megaliths, dolmens, heathered hills, bagpipes, rainbows, and friends . . .

I don't know why—amnesia, DNA, personal history, Donna—but my good, positive, and happy memories and thoughts outnumber the rest. I see loss, feel it, and move on. For a "glass is half empty" guy, it's a miracle.

Of course, I haven't begun the real decline yet, the non compos mentis. Who knows how I'll feel then? If I remain lucky, I'll live like my mom to ninety-seven, 872 years fewer than Methuselah, twenty-eight more than my dad, with all my marbles, doing the Monday to Sunday *New York Times* crossword in ink, winning at Scrabble without cheating, going to the theater, restaurants, museums, and concerts, accompanied by family and friends who like me and want to be with me. And if not, I hope no one tells me, and I'm the last to know.

I want to be like my major professor, friend, and mentor, Ken Dolbeare, who at the end of his life wanted to return to Hispanic culture, where he'd been living for years in Colombia. He wanted to go to Mexico to be near the sea and his ex-wife, the last lady love of his life. He was ninety and frail and couldn't make the trip, so he journeyed in his head. He started speaking Spanish and went there, and I hope he was there and young and healthy and in love, on the sea, a Navy man, speaking fluently and happy, because that's how I want to be—back at my fiftieth birthday party with Donna, my mom, Yvonne and her family, Jean and Sharon, and all my French and American family and friends, mastering well-conjugated, gender-correct, New York-California-Breton-accented French, finally able to say and proclaim, "*délicieux.*" Delicious.

I want to be with Donna, her marker next to mine, like two pillows on a bed of Monsieur Charles's moleless lawn, under the hawthorn tree Donna and I planted near the stone wall everyone thought was mine, facing the river-canal and Yvonne's once-upon-a-time garden, beneath Brittany's luminous sky, and a granite marker that says:

Monsieur Greenseed,
Un homme drôle et écrivain, A funny man and writer
Il se plaît tellement ici, He likes it so much here
Il est resté, He stayed

It's a paradox my French friends and neighbors will appreciate: when I'm finally, finally gone, I'll finally, finally be here, finally French.

P.S.

21 Things I Learned About Brittany, France, and Me

1. Politeness, courtesy—*politesse*—matters: saying hello and goodbye; cheek kissing, one to four times, depending on the person, place, and occasion; saying please and thank you, which I always pronounce *mercy*, and mean it.

2. Behavior matters: kindness, thoughtfulness, saying the right thing, *doing* the right thing, being *gentile*, which in France I think of as gentle and nice, and in the U.S. as not being Jewish.

3. *Vous* and *tu* matter: *vous* is the formal way to address "you." *Tu* is the informal. Think of the old days, which are never far away in France, and a silent Mister and Missus, like, *comment allez-vous*, how are you (Monsieur/Madame)?—as opposed to *comment vas-tu*, how's it going? In the U.S., I'm Mister Informal. In France, I'm *vous-vousing* all the way, because there's

237

little going wrong with *vous*, and lots with *tu*—and given the number of ways I do go wrong, I need to cut my losses, so here's looking at *vous*, kid, because *tu* is too familiar and personal to say.

4. Appearance matters: clothes, skin, hair, shoes, eye-glasses. It's good to be *chic* in France, something I've, unfortunately, never, ever been accused of. The closest I've come to *chic* is cheeky, and it isn't close.

5. Rules matter: there are bazillions of them, a gazillion of which I'll never know or understand, like gender in grammar, and where to place my knife and fork to indicate I'm done eating. In France, it's always best to follow the rules, until, of course, it's not. The trick is to know when and how to break them, a trick I'll never master, so unlike in the U.S., where I prefer to lead, in France, I follow—except when it comes to language. There, I violate conventions wantonly, which is not the same as willfully. For foreigners like me, of whom little is expected, this is acceptable. For French people, it's social death.

6. Time matters: not present time, of course. *That's* irrelevant, even for SNCF and Air France. In the U.S., time is measured in minutes and seconds, in France, decades and centuries. In France, the past never goes away: today is not the first day of the rest of your life; yesterday is probably better than today, and definitely better than tomorrow. In the U.S., where new is better than old, and old is practically new, the goal is to disrupt and break with the past. In France, the old is always present and usually valued: the goal isn't to break from the past, but to continue it. Think of waves and particles. In the

U.S., every event is a point, a particle, a place of potential departure and take-off. In France, events are part of a large human wave, the tsunami of history, which is probably why arriving at 8:40 for an eight o'clock dinner doesn't matter to anyone but an American host.

7. Money matters: French people say it doesn't, but it does. In the U.S., I know money is important and acknowledge it. I have friends who figure their cost of a meal, including tax and tip, to the penny, their portion of gas used on a trip to the ounce and penny. It's straight, simple, and clear. Not in France. In France, people don't want to talk about money even though they do. In France, it's a whispered, under-the-table, sotto voce topic. In the U.S., it is *the* topic. In the U.S., the waiter puts the bill on my table before I'm done eating. In France, I can't get the bill—or the waiter—even when I ask, *especially* when I ask . . .

8. French people say *normal* and *en principe* (in principle) the way Americans say "ordinarily," each of which lets me know when I hear it to expect the unusual, extra-ordinary, exceptional, usually for the worse. For example, if someone says to me, "Ordinarily, normally, in principle, this tape will hold this wire in place long enough for you to drive home, alone, at night, in the rain. . . . Sign here. . . ." I won't and don't—in any language.

9. Disagreement is a way of life in France, and one of the rules of living. To differ is not a breach, but a bond. In the U.S., we seek to agree, especially when we disagree. In France, people disagree even if they agree, which means I never know if I'm hearing an argument, a love-fest, or both.

10. *On parle anglais ici,* English is spoken here: more and more it is—and spoken well. French people are speaking more and better English, actually even willing and wanting to do so, which is odd, because now that Brexit is law, fewer English people are coming to France. It's another of those French paradoxes: fewer English, more English. It's too bad for Brits, but great for monolingual Americans, like me.

11. *C'est la vie,* that's life: French people are not generally an optimistic, positive people. They await the unwelcome, and when it comes, *"C'est la vie"* is the response. In the U.S., the response is, "Shit happens." In the U.S., I fight hubris: how else could I have written five books? In France, it's abasement: how many times can I fail? Let me count the ways. If I had all these failures in the U.S., I'd take it personally and be depressed and angry—shit happens—but I've been in Brittany and France long enough to know it's not personal, just life, *c'est la vie.*

12. Family is the basic social unit in France, not the individual. If Marie and David are coming for dinner, I expect them to bring Felix, Lucie, and Louise, their kids, and if they have a dog, maybe him/her, too. As host, it's my job to have food (all seven courses) and drink (from apéritif to digestif) for all of them, and something for the dog, too.

13. I shop at the mom-and-pop stores to support friends and neighbors and to avoid listeria, salmonella, E. coli, shigella, botulism, and allergic reactions to something added and not identified on the package, because every week there are more *supermarché* recalls, as French food

is becoming as industrial as American food. . . . For household items and appliances, I've learned the expensive way that French-made products too often look better than they work. Take my thermos and vacuum, for example . . . Please . . .

14. Being a fool or foolish or made fun of is funny and okay for an American (like me) in France, but not for a French person. *Sometimes*, French people can make fun of other French people, like Jews can make fun of Jews, and non-Jews can't. In the U.S., saying the wrong thing to the wrong person at the wrong time and place can get you shot. In France, it will get you ostracized, which is the social equivalent of being dead. In France, the joke is always on me—or me.

15. In the U.S., I worry about the big things: climate change, civil and not-so-civil wars, affordable housing, crumbling infrastructure, racism, poverty, disease, and traffic. In France, the big things are beyond me, and it's the little things that torment, like guessing what word to turn the dial to on my new clothes dryer to rapidly dry not-so-dirty cottons, and what to serve Bruno and Françoise for dinner. It's the difference between looking through a telescope the correct way and the wrong way. In the U.S., I look the right way and blemishes seem larger, closer, and more immediate, and I get angry and upset. In France, I look the wrong way and everything seems smaller, farther away, and precious, and I feel nostalgic and protective.

16. In the U.S., my life in retirement is semi-public. In France, I'm fully exposed. In the U.S., I am what I do—or did—a teacher of history, political science,

and English, a union guy, and a writer. In France, I'm Popeye: I yam what I yam what I am—and that's all I yam.

17. I recently saw the movie *Casablanca* for the zillionth time and was surprised that my favorite scene has changed. It used to be about righteous triumph, when Victor Laszlo says, "Play 'The Marseillaise'! Play it!" and drowns out the Germans singing "Die Wacht am Rhein." Now, it's about amity, when Rick and Louis walk off together, France and the U.S., arm in arm, like the good old days, as I once imagined them.

18. I used to be an "Imagine" guy. Now, I'm "Life is what happens to you while you're busy making other plans." I believe everything changes, and nothing does. I have great expectations and none. It's a conundrum, but as long as life goes on—mine and friends and family and earth's, the universe and its people—I can't complain too much, though Donna says I can.

19. More and more as I get older, I know how much of life—*my* life—has been luck: genetic luck, geographic luck, historical luck, biological luck, love luck, and dumb luck, and in my case in France, *very* dumb luck. I hope to heaven it continues and lasts.

20. And I know this, too: life without great food, good wine, friends, family, five-week vacations, healthy pensions, generous medical care, many holidays, passion, engagement, and a safety net as tall and wide as the sky is not worth living, and is not French—and I am happy and thankful to enjoy and experience it . . . .

21. Born in the U.S.A., DNA from Europe: my grandparents were born in Hungary, Poland, Russia, and

Ukraine, and my father in Hungary. When he was one, his family moved from Budapest to Strasbourg to be near his mother's favorite sister, Pepe, who married a French man. French was probably my dad's first formal language. France is definitely where he first went to school. At age nine, he and my grandmother left France from Marseilles to join my grandfather in New York City, where he went a year before. This was in the late 1920s. Now, almost one hundred years later, I'm back to where my grandparents and theirs before them and those before them started, a particle in the wave of history, wanting, searching, and finding a good life, a *very* good and lucky life, in deed.

Mercy beaucoup.

P.P.S.

. . . I decided to paint my shutters royal blue after the forest green, and after that burnt umber, and after that I'll buy new oak shutters and varnish the wood, and after that. . . . It's the best kept secret in the universe. . . . Everyone has their hopes and their prayers, and nobody—not even Methuselah— knows. . . .

https://www.markgreenside.com/blue-shutters
Photo by Norbert Uzseka

Appreciations and Thanks

To those who shared their lives, words, and skills with me and helped make this book, and those who read the final drafts and made it better:

Kim Addonizio, Hélène and Jacques Ascoet, Rolland Autret, Yvonne, Joe, Patrice, Thierry, Christine, Estel, and Marion Bastard, Eric Behar, Albine Belinger, Louise Benn and Martin Brett, Val and Alan Bennett, Louis-Charles Billior, Xavier and Martine Bourret, Charles Castan, Timmie Chandler, Marcel, Eric, and Laure Claude, Ella, Rick, and Jacob Cole, Michelle Cooper and Dominique Kermoal, Yvette Creff, Loni, Bob, and Karen Dantzler and Eric Lilavois, Yvon Derrien, Marie Donal, Christiane Dupuis and Jacky Link, Taryn Fagerness, Christian Foix, Norma and Augie Francesco, Matthieu Gapihan, Jocelyne Gaubert and Pierrick Le Therizen, Roy Glassberg, Yvonne, Georges, and Gilles Goulard, Tatjana, Ael, and Emil Goulard-Lomic, Sylvie and Alain Gourret, Jeff and Corinne Greenside, Bob Grill, Anne Hascoet, E. Sherman Hayman, Annie and Claude Jourdren, Jean-Pierre Juguet and family, Andrew Juris, Marie-Luce, Alain, and Pauline

Kerdreux, Jean-Yves and Catherine Kernarc, Henry Kletter, Danuta and Marshall Krantz, Marie Lambert, Bruno and Françoise Lamezec and Ludovic, Stéphanie, Erine, and Victor Pochard-Lamezec and Naomi Caraes, Bob and Christiane Le Lionnais, Mary Lavor and Aldo and Flavio Petrazzi, Jean-Pierre, Joëlle, Gaël, and Marie Le Meitour and David Le Carrer, Jean-Claude L' Homme, Rob Liddiard, Mac Dan, Emmanuel Maho, Malgorzata Maruszkin, Leslie Meredith, Tom Myers and Lauren Schaffer, Michel and Yvette Ogier, Laurie and Danny Paige, Paula Panich, Sophie Picon and Dominique Ould-Ferhat, Warren and Janice Poland, François Quiniou, Harry Rabin, Daniela Rapp, Deborah Ritchken, Sharon, Jean, Yann, and Noé Rival, Olivier, Catherine, Tanguy, Paul, Hervé, Emilie, and Elise Roche, Sidonie Sawyer, Fred Setterberg and Ann Van Steenberg, Phillip and Anne-Lise Spitzer, Chris and John Stallard, Kim Thoman and Bob Bezemek, Michel, Francine, Gerard, and Marie-Thérèse Tricore, Norbert Uzseka, Fred and Muriel Vasseur, Béatrice and Jean-Jacques Vierne, George and Marion Wallach, Eric Weiss and Misty Lucas.